BALTIMORE AFIRE

REVISED EDITION

BALTIMORE AFIRE

Being an account of one of AMERICA'S GREAT CONFLAGRATIONS

which in two days in February, 1904

wiped out practically the entire business district of

BALTIMORE, MARYLAND

—and containing a TRIBUTE

to the courage and resourcefulness of the city's businessmen

who REBUILT *a* NEW *and* BETTER CITY

on the ashes of an old one

by HAROLD A. WILLIAMS

With a New Epilogue and Additional Illustrations

Printed on the SEVENTY-FIFTH ANNIVERSARY of that Great Fire by—

SCHNEIDEREITH & SONS

Baltimore, Maryland 21230

First edition — Copyright 1954

Revised edition — Copyright 1979

SCHNEIDEREITH & SONS

Printers and Publishers

BALTIMORE, MARYLAND 21230

International Standard Book Number 0-9602304-1-6

BALTIMORE'S GREAT FIRE

T HIS BOOK IS DEDICATED TO THE BUSINESSMEN OF *Old Baltimore who did not despair in the dark winter of 1904 when their offices and shops lay in smoking ruins from the Great Fire, but who faced the uncertain future with a faith, courage and resourcefulness that made possible the Baltimore of today. Their great faith and determination have become an essential part of the tradition of this 250-year-old city. Their unquenchable spirit will always be an inspiration to its citizens and builders.*

FORWARD!

ON MONDAY, February 8, 1904—while the fire still raged in down-town Baltimore—*The Sun* declared on its front page, "There is little doubt that many men, formerly prosperous, will be ruined by the events of the past 24 hours . . . Many of the spectators saw their all go up in flames before their eyes, and there were men with hopeless faces and despairing expression on every hand. They stood around usually in dazed silence and only occasionally would a word of despair be heard. That they were disheartened was apparent to the casual observer . . ."

But these men were not disheartened for long. On February 10, *The Sun,* in a three column headline, proclaimed:

To Build A New And Greater Baltimore
Business Men And Financiers Will Meet Today
Not Appalled By Disaster

And disaster it was—the greatest one ever to strike the 175-year-old city. Over 1,500 buildings in the downtown district were burned down or out. Damage was estimated between $125,000,000 and $150,000,000.

While fires still burned sporadically in the devastated section, an area covering almost 140 acres, the businessmen met to plan for the future. The tremendous task of reconstruction began while smoke was still rising from the debris. The newspapers began talking about the "indomitable pluck and ingenuity" of Baltimoreans.

At first the work went slowly. But it gathered momentum as the streets were cleared and widened. Three years after the fire, Blanchard Randall, president of the Merchants and Manufacturers Association of Baltimore, announced, "The great changes in our city are not yet all accomplished facts, but our people are more busy than they were: wages are better; sales are larger. General business conditions are quite equal to what they were before the fire and in many branches improved . . . The city is to be more healthful, more beautiful and more prosperous . . ."

Out of the ashes of an old city, through the courage and resourcefulness of its people, a new and greater Baltimore was in the making.

FIRE! FIRE! FIRE!

DOOMSDAY

T HE FEBRUARY SKY was overcast and there was a brisk wind blowing across Baltimore from the southwest. The mild weather the day before had melted most of a recent snow, but there was still muddy slush at the crossings. A hint of rain was in the air. About the only people on the street were church-goers—it was a Sunday. As the wind swept across the cobblestone streets men clutched their derbies and women held tight to their broad-brimmed hats and their long skirts. The talk was about the weather. Practically everyone agreed that it was going to be a miserable day.

The day did not promise much other than a leisurely dinner and the Sunday papers, which dwelt on the possibility of war between Japan and Russia, and the serious illness of Mark Hanna, the famous Senator from Ohio, who was attended by Dr. William Osler, of the Hopkins. About the only events scheduled for that afternoon and evening were a memorial service by the Baltimore Aerie of the Fraternal Order of Eagles at the Maryland Theater, and a talk by the secretary of the American United Presbyterian Church at the Opera House.

Baltimore on that February 7, 1904 was looking forward to a quiet Sunday at home.

Then a fire started in a six-story brick building, occupied by the dry-goods firm of John E. Hurst & Company, that stood between Hopkins Place and Liberty on the south side of German (now Redwood) Street.

The first alarm sounded at 10:48 a.m. It was an automatic alarm—one set to go off by heat. No. 2 Truck Company, No. 15 Engine Company, the

1

Seventeen minutes after the first alarm. This photograph shows the six-story Hurst Building already a seething ruin. A tremendous smoke explosion hurtled the flames and heavy firebrands across the streets into four other buildings.

2

Salvage Corps, and Fifth District Engineer L. H. Burkhardt responded. As Captain John Kahl raced up Liberty Street with his No. 15 Engine Company he saw wisps of smoke coming from the top windows of the Hurst Building. But still it did not look like much of a blaze. As soon as he reached the scene he checked the automatic alarm box on the side of the building. It indicated that the fire was in the basement. Firemen smashed the glass doors on the German Street side and entered with a ¾-inch chemical line and a 2½-inch water hose. Standing on the stairway to the basement they could see flames drawing across the basement ceiling to the elevator shaft. There was only a little smoke on the first floor and in the basement, where fire seemed to be burning in packing cases. As Captain Kahl, the first officer to enter the building, stood on the stairway directing the hose, he heard doors slamming throughout the upper floors. He first thought that a watchman was closing them. Suddenly there was a downpour of smoke through the elevator shaft and then the building and the ground shook. It was a smoke explosion, but at the time it was believed to have been caused by gasoline. The impact blew off the roof and broke the windows. Flames shot out with a loud whistling noise. Heavy firebrands were thrown across the narrow street—only about fifty feet wide—into adjoining buildings whose windows were broken by the concussion.

The explosion occurred about five minutes after the alarm sounded.

Firemen in the building somehow managed to escape. But the flames swept out over the fire tower of No. 15 Engine Company, which was drawing into position on Liberty Street, and singed a fire horse, Goliath, who, because of his injuries, was to become one of the best known horses in Baltimore. The lashing flames and the firebrands soon ignited a steamer and a fire truck standing on German Street. They could not be reached because of the heat. Hostlers had removed the horses a few minutes earlier to go back to the stations for additional apparatus.

By this time two more alarms had been sounded. At 10:51 someone, probably an officer of the Salvage Corps, pulled Box 447, at Baltimore and Liberty Streets, and at 10:55 District Engineer Burkhardt ran to Box 414, at German and Howard Streets, to sound the "four twos"— a third alarm.

3

140 ACRES OF DESTRUCTION

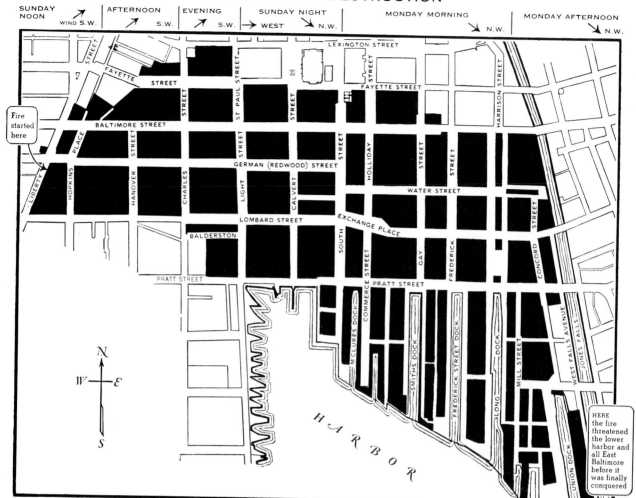

PROGRESS OF THE FIRE

The fire started in the Hurst Building which stood on the south side of German Street at Liberty. Smoke explosions flared it west and south, but fresh winds from the southwest carried the broad front of the blaze to the northeast. By 5 p.m. much of the area between Fayette and German Streets and west of Charles was in flames or already burned. At 7.30 p.m. the wind changed to the west, hurrying the ragged eastern edges of the fire toward St. Paul Street where buildings caught fire by 9 o'clock. The skyscrapers in the vicinity of Baltimore and Calvert Streets were afire around 10. This intersection was probably the hottest spot in town, temperatures reaching an estimated 2,500 degrees.

At 11 p.m. the wind changed to the northwest and reached a maximum velocity of 30 miles an hour. At that time flames were racing down Baltimore Street as far as South Street and cutting through the financial district in a southeasterly direction toward the waterfront.

At 3 a.m. on Monday, the southern edge of the fire, which had been checked along Lombard Street, finally crossed Charles and moved down to Pratt Street. By 4 a.m. the north side of Pratt was blazing almost to Jones Falls. By some quirk of wind, one tip of the fire turned at the Falls and went rushing back to the west almost to Cheapside through the dock area.

A last-ditch fight was made along the Falls with thirty-seven fire engines. By 11 a.m. fire had destroyed practically everything to the Falls from Baltimore Street to the tip of Union Dock. Carried by the northwest wind, sparks started dangerous blazes on the *east side of the stream* in the vicinity of Union Dock but these were contained and conquered. The Great Fire was under control by 5 p.m. Monday.

4

George W. Horton, chief engineer of the Fire Department, arrived from home shortly after 11 o'clock. He stood for a few minutes on German Street, west of Liberty, estimating the situation. Crackling flames spurted from three sides of the Hurst Building, which was obviously doomed. The fire had jumped from the southeast corner of Liberty and German Streets to the building of Carr, Owens & Heineman, a wholesale drug company, on the northwest corner. From there it leaped east to the National Exchange Bank on the northeast corner and across to the northeast corner of German and Hopkins Place. Four buildings were burning fiercely and many others were beginning to burn. Chief Horton directed the placement of hose lines for several minutes and then hurried on to make a quick survey, walking around the spreading edges of the fire. Before he had finished he decided to appeal to the Washington Fire Department for assistance, the first of many out-of-town departments called upon that day. On Baltimore Street he met Police Lieut. Charles M. Cole who was asked to send the message. Cole's telegram, which was received in Washington at 11:40 a.m., read, "Desperate fire here. Must have help at once."

Chief Horton then met Pinkney W. Wilkinson, secretary to the Fire Commissioners, and he ordered Wilkinson to summon all companies. Wilkinson ran to the Salvage Corps Station on Liberty Street at Fayette and telephoned the chief operator at fire headquarters, on the first floor of the City Hall, to sound the general alarm which would bring everything in service. When the distress signal rang in the fire stations some desk men thought the call was caused accidentally by a short circuit, and they double-checked the alarm.

Only a few people, most of them on their way to church, were in the downtown section around 11 o'clock. But the galloping fire horses, the clanging engines and the smoke explosion soon drew many who came running and shouting from all directions. Soon they stood ten to twenty deep across some of the streets leading to the fire. Before police could set up fire lines they pressed close to equipment and made it difficult for firemen to bring bushels of coal from the fuel wagons to the steamers.

The first spectators regarded the fire as an exhilarating sight. Some even brought babies and children who were held up to get a better look.

Flames gutting the large building of Guggenheimer, Weil & Company, printers, on the north-east corner of Lombard and Liberty Streets, illuminate the windows and send great clouds of smoke billowing over the downtown area. The Sutton Building, on the right, did not burn.

But the mood changed and the crowd grew as the fire spread through the substantial brick buildings and warehouses occupied by clothing manufacturers, drug, drygoods and liquor companies. Children and babies were taken home. Women cried when flames ate into the buildings where they worked. Men, despite warnings from police and firemen, rushed into burning buildings, or buildings about to burn, to retrieve money from their safes or records from their desks. Some had their clothing scorched by flaming paper and wood that dropped suddenly on them. Others were injured when the tumbling walls of the Hurst Building splattered in the streets. The falling embers and crashing walls drove many away. Others bolted after Hopkins Place was rocked by an explosion. It was caused by a magazine filled with gunpowder owned by Findlay, Roberts & Co. which, in compliance with fire regulations, was stored on the sidewalk.

The explosion, which sent flames shooting in all directions, gave impetus to the fire already fanned by a twelve-mile-per-hour wind from

The losing battle of the firemen is graphically illustrated here. They pour three streams of water on a smoking building while just a few doors away the flames have gutted and burst the walls of two large buildings. The scene is on Liberty near German Street.

Street crowds along the sidewalk cheered. The Washingtonians were assigned to Little Sharp Street. Their hoses would not fit the Baltimore hydrants so they wrapped them to the plugs with canvas bandages. The streams were so weak that the men had to hold the nozzles dangerously close to the flames.

Baltimore firemen, their clothes scorched by sparks or drenched with water, were not doing much better. They would risk their lives to get hoses on buildings just catching fire, but before they could soak the interior, fire would shoot out of the structure from top to bottom, driving the men away. Some claimed that pouring water on the buildings was the same as dousing them with gasoline. The heat was converting many of the streams into steam which intensified the flames.

11

A number of firemen were treated along the fire lines by Fire Department surgeons and private physicians for minor cuts, smoke inhalation and electric shocks from falling wires. One of the few who had to be removed from the scene was cut about the face by a bursting hose. A police captain, Bernard Ward, was burned about the neck as the intense heat ignited his celluloid collar. He immediately ordered his men to take off their collars.

Although many spectators helped firemen hurriedly move hose from abandoned positions, much of it was buried under collapsing walls or covered by jumbled live wires that had dropped from splintered or burning poles. George W. Gail, president of the Board of Fire Commissioners, told Wilkinson to "Get more hose. Get all the hose you can." The secretary to the board telephoned officials of three companies in New York and ordered 60,000 feet. The first consignment, 10,000 feet, arrived Monday at Calvert Station coiled in the aisles of passenger cars.

It was difficult, if not impossible, for Acting Chief Emrich to direct the general strategy of the battle, which by early afternoon covered nearly twelve blocks and was leaping into new territory every minute.

Emrich tried to direct his forces by sending word to the district engineers spread around the perimeter of the fire, but often his tactics were made obsolete by the sudden outbreak of fire in new areas. Emrich said at one point, "We are in the hands of God." Most of the direction was done by captains at the company level who maneuvered their men and equipment as best they could.

At every building, at every street corner, it was a losing battle. Firemen who had a hard time putting out one small blaze were fighting a giant that could swoop through an entire block and destroy it without difficulty. A company would be assigned to pour water into a building starting to burn. Before the hoses were in position the men were fighting a fire in not one building but ten. One of the most pitiful sights of the fire—and one that convinced many a spectator that Baltimore was doomed—was to see an entire block—including the telephone poles—blazing fiercely while several lonely-looking firemen with inadequate hose attempted to check the irresistible flames.

Emrich's most effective strategy was the withdrawal of equipment

Behind a thick, black wall of smoke that engulfs Hanover Street, the spreading fire pushes toward Lombard Street while firemen attempt to beat it back with the only hose they could connect. Fire hydrants were fewer in those days, and debris from falling walls covered many.

from the fire lines for dispersal throughout the city to combat subsidiary blazes. During the first twenty-four hours of the fire, fifty-two box alarms were sounded for blazes started by embers which flew through the air like flaming arrows. Sparks started a small fire on the Zion Lutheran Church near the City Hall, at the old Front Street Theater and on buildings east of the Falls. Tar roofs, awnings, even grape arbors, were blazing all over town and householders were kept busy putting them out. The roofs of the City Hall, Court House, Post Office, and other public buildings, were guarded by bucket brigades and sweepers.

In the middle of the afternoon Mayor McLane and Harry W. Rodgers, his secretary, appeared at Hanover and Lombard Streets as the east side of Hanover began to catch fire. After a consultation with fire officials the

13

mayor ordered police to drive the crowd back beyond Light Street on the east and Pratt Street on the south. The intention was to dynamite the block bounded by Hanover, German, Charles and Lombard Streets.

The first wagon load of dynamite—1,000 pounds, covered with dirt—came from Anne Arundel County. It was parked for over an hour on Lombard Street between Hanover and Charles while firemen attempted to halt the blaze. Authorities were still reluctant to use explosives.

Word of the plan to blow up buildings spread rapidly. When it reached a stalled line of teamsters who were trying to drive their over-loaded wagons out of an alley off Charles Street they became panic-stricken. Each one tried to beat the other out. There was a sudden entanglement of wagons, rearing horses and shouting, cursing drivers. It took police a half hour to empty the one-block-long alley.

The dynamiting began about 5 p.m. It was done under the supervision of City Engineer Fendall by Roy E. Lafferty, a demolition expert who had worked for the Government at Fort Carroll, assisted by C. R. Weaver, H. A. Albert and a crew of army sappers. The bustle of the crew and the strange equipment created curiosity among the spectators and many broke through the police lines to see what was going on. They fell back only when police shouted, "Dynamite! Dynamite! Go. Go!" When some-one yelled, "The fuse is lit! Run!" the curious fell over one another in getting out of the way.

The building occupied by John Duer & Sons on Charles Street south of German was one of the first to be dynamited. It was already on fire in the rear when the crew, carrying the dynamite in buckets, planted fifty sticks in the basement, attached a fuse and ran a wire from it to the battery, several hundred feet away. One of the experts said he hoped the charge "would drive the foundations from under the building and bring it toppling to the ground." The detonation made a tremendous noise, shook the ground and broke a great many windows—but the build-ing remained standing.

Another and heavier charge was laid at the Schwab Brothers Building on the southwest corner of Charles and German Streets. The only damage it did was to bore a big hole in the ground. A few minutes later the entire row of buildings the experts had planned to blow up was engulfed by fire.

14

Firebrands, carried by the strong winds, ignite the roof of the building third from the corner. Firemen are unable to force the streams of water above the second floor. The awning on the right was burned by a heavy downpour of sparks

15

Later the crews dynamited a dozen or more structures on Charles, Lombard and Baltimore Streets but except in one or two cases the walls did not crumble and the buildings remained as fuel for the flames. After watching the futile effects of their work, there was some talk among the crews of substituting cannon from Fort McHenry.

But the cannon were far away and the dynamite was at hand (about 3,000 additional pounds had been brought from quarries or contributed by contractors and the Northern Central Railway), so the tired men worked on, attempting to stop the fire but often only succeeding in spreading it. About 7 p.m., after dynamiting two or three buildings on West Fayette Street, they planted their explosives in the department store of J. W. Putts & Co., on the southwest corner of Charles and Fayette Streets. They hoped to smother the blaze coming up fast from the west and the south. The explosion hit the Fayette Street side of the building and drove firebrands across into the Hall and Headington structure on the northwest corner. The blast also shattered windows in the Union Trust Building on the northeast corner. Soon that massive building was ablaze. Firemen had been hoping that it would serve as a fire wall.

Officials wanted to dynamite O'Neill's, just to the north of Hall and Headington, but Thomas O'Neill, a redheaded Irishman who owned the department store, protested vehemently. He stood on the first floor proclaiming that if his store were blown up he would be blown up with it. The authorities could not budge him, and the plan was abandoned. O'Neill's determination kept the building standing. His unique sprinkler system and an improvised lake probably saved it from the fire. On the rear windows were T-shaped nozzles that dropped a curtain of water so thick that the flames could not penetrate it. To guard against falling brands and sparks, employees opened the water tank atop the building and flooded the roof by plugging the downspouts.

Another trick was used by employees of the Lloyd L. Jackson Company, at Liberty and Lombard Streets. They took every blanket from the well-stocked storerooms and, after wetting them with water from the roof tank, spread them across the top of the building and hung them from cornices. The wet coverings helped save the building.

From Liberty to Charles Street the roar of the flames was so great that

The fire devours everything in sight. Brick buildings, telephone poles, electric wires—even the streets—are burning. The firemen, armed with one insignificant hose, can do little more than watch the terrible but magnificent spectacle.

it sounded like wind howling on a mountain top. Buildings were burning on both sides of Fayette Street under a pyrotechnic shower of sparks that gave the street an eerie but fairyland effect. Baltimore Street, with stores and offices flaming from basements to roofs, looked like a gigantic fiery furnace. German and Lombard Streets were rivers of flame. Between the northern and southern edges of the expanding fire, wooden blocks and asphalt took fire so that the street beds of downtown Baltimore were actually aflame.

The flames were irresistible. Fire walls did not stop them. Wide spaces between buildings did not stop them. Dynamite did not stop them. They just pushed on and on. Modern three- and four-story brick buildings—built, the architects said, to withstand anything—fell as easily as dilapidated wooden sheds. A fireman, who probably did not know what the word irresistible meant, described the force and fury of the fire perfectly. "A thousand fire companies couldn't stop it," he said. "Tonight the fire is king." King it was.

A spectator on the top floor of the Belvedere Hotel said that the smoke and flames looked like some fiery demon. He was struck by the fact that there was a terrific onrush of flames just as the church bells were chiming the calls for evening service. Another, looking at the statue of George Washington atop the monument in Mount Vernon Place, said, "The Father of our country looks like Nero gloating over the destruction of Rome." A companion added, "All he needs is a fiddle."

Between 6 and 7 p.m., Police Commissioner Upshur requested Brig. Gen. Lawrason Riggs to call out units of the Maryland National Guard to assist the police. The Board of Police Commissioners had exercised this authority only once before—for the railroad riots in 1877.

General Riggs' order of assembly to the commanding officers of the Fourth and Fifth Regiments read, "You will assemble your regiment at your armory and hold it in readiness for further orders. Fatigue uniforms, leggings, overcoats, camp hats and pouch. Supply horses for three ambulances and put in charge of your Hospital Corps." Men were summoned by telephone and the repeated tolling of the City Hall bell three times—a signal for assembly.

Later that evening the commandant of the Army garrison at Fort

18

Guided by a strong but veering wind, the fire made many strange turns. It just lapped at the Court House and missed the Post Office but completely destroyed nearby buildings. This view at Calvert and Fayette Streets is from the Court House steps toward the southeast.

McHenry telephoned Marshal Farnan to ask if assistance was needed. The marshal replied that government buildings were threatened. Thirty men were dispatched immediately on horseback. Armed with fixed bayonets they first formed a line across Fayette Street at Calvert. Later they guarded the Post Office, the Sub-Treasury and the Custom House.

Before midnight more than 2,000 soldiers and sailors were on duty. The Fifth Regiment, Col. Henry M. Warfield, commanding, supplied 800; so did the Fourth Regiment, Col. Willard Howard, commanding. Troop A, led by Capt. Joseph W. Shirley, supplied 200, as did the Naval Reserves under the command of Lieut. E. G. Willard.

The Board of Police Commissioners placed the military under the

19

immediate direction of General Riggs. The soldiers had charge, for the most part, of the fire territory. The Baltimore police protected the rest of the city with a force of 750 patrolmen, 129 squad sergeants, twenty-five detectives, nineteen lieutenants and nine captains.

Police and soldiers were kept busy. They held back frenzied men who were bent on searching for safes in the wreckage. At gun point they ordered others from buildings about to burn, and they checked burning buildings to make sure everyone was out. They tried to keep hundreds of "rescue" wagons and carts moving through the growing crowds and around the stalled trolleys that were banked up on the outskirts of the fire. They tried to subdue drunken men. They helped the tiring firemen move hose and haul coal from the fuel wagons and they gave directions to out-of-town firemen who had been ordered to proceed to new locations.

Assisting the Baltimore Fire Department in addition to the Washington contingents were units and men from Baltimore and Anne Arundel Counties, Philadelphia, Wilmington, York and Altoona. Most of them made the trips to Baltimore on special trains, and all were cheered as they took up their positions on the fire lines. Many companies could not attach their hoses to Baltimore plugs because of differences in coupling sizes. But the men fought long and valiantly.

It was a terrible, hectic, chaotic night. Nothing stopped the flames, nobody knew how to stop them, and no one knew when they would stop. The sky over downtown Baltimore was blotted out by smoke. Fire seemed to be everywhere. The continued tolling of the City Hall bell calling out the militia underscored the feeling of urgency, of desperation and of doom.

The dormitory of No. 6 Engine House, which had been converted into an emergency hospital, was packed with firemen suffering from gashes and burns. Volunteer nurses were putting new arrivals on the engine house floor. Old fire buffs said that the scene reminded them of an army field hospital during the Civil War.

Governor Edwin Warfield arrived from Annapolis at 10:15 p.m. He had planned to come up on the special train that left at 8 o'clock with the Annapolis Fire Company, but he missed it. He asked for, and got,

20

The hottest spot in town—firemen estimated that the blaze here developed 2,500 degrees of heat. From left to right, the Maryland Trust, the B. & O. and Continental Trust Buildings. The sixteen-story "completely fireproof" Continental, tallest in Baltimore, burned like a torch.

another special train which rushed him to Baltimore with his staff.

Fifty wagon loads of mail were removed from the Post Office to the Pennsylvania Avenue and Waverly substations. Passing men and women helped carry out archives and records from the Court House. Telephone operators, who had stayed at their posts in the St. Paul Street exchange wrapped in water-soaked blankets as protection against sparks, finally were driven from their switchboards.

Crowds stood huddled in the downtown section east of St. Paul Street—close to the guardsmen in the bright light of the fire or on dark street corners blocks away. The electric lights on Pratt Street were out but it still was a main thoroughfare for sightseers. Anyone who moved

21

about was splattered with mud thrown up by passing wagons from the wet and dirty streets. Everyone was listening hungrily for news. News supported by facts was hard to get. But there were plenty of rumors. One, that the fire was under control, had been picked up by a press association that afternoon and flashed to other cities. There were rumors that Chief Horton, who had suffered a minor shock, was fatally injured. There was a rumor that Marshal Farnan had been killed. There was another that John M. Hood, president of the United Railway and Electric Company, was missing. His friends searched through the ruins, looking for his body, and then found him, alive in a St. Paul Street office discussing plans with his superintendent. There were many rumors about people being consumed by flames and firemen crushed by falling walls. False reports about firemen were so prevalent that some firemen sneaked home to tell their families they were all right. One report that turned out to be true concerned the evacuation of patients from City Hospital (now Mercy Hospital) on Calvert Street. Three hundred patients, including eighteen women and two babies who had been transferred from the Maryland Maternity and Lying-In Hospital on Lombard Street earlier in the day, were removed in city and regimental ambulances to Johns Hopkins, Maryland General, St. Joseph's and University Hospitals. Patients who were in a critical condition were completely covered so they would not see what was going on about them.

After the Union Trust Building caught fire the blaze moved east through the smaller structures to the Herald Building on the northwest corner of St. Paul and Fayette Streets. Shortly before 9 p.m. the newspaper staff abandoned their offices followed by their twenty-four-year-old city editor, Henry L. Mencken. The blaze paused at the Herald property but before long fire was on the roof and smoke was billowing from the pressroom. The Law Office Building and the Condon Buildings, which adjoined on St. Paul Street, were also afire. It looked as if the Court House, just across the street, was doomed. Furniture, books, even the drapes, were taken from the city court room, on the Fayette and St. Paul Street corner, to the juvenile court in the middle of the Court House. Other records were pushed into the vaults. The floors in many places were covered with dirt and the roof was strewn with cinders.

DEVASTATION

MOST BALTIMOREANS were up all night, watching, waiting, praying. Many of those living near the downtown area put children to bed with their clothes on and then stood anxiously at windows or on rooftops as lookouts for flying sparks. Thousands gathered on the hills of Highlandtown, on the ridges of Druid Hill Park, and on the slopes and walks of Federal Hill. For protection against the strong winds and the February night air they wrapped themselves in blankets. The sky above them was mockingly clear and blue, sprinkled with stars, but over the fire area it was blotted with smoke which at times was shaped by the wind into a great attenuated cone. The eyes on Federal Hill were caught by the fast-rising, swirling sparks, by the great tongues of leaping flames, and, one of the prettiest sights of all, by the dull gleam of the fire reflected from the wet, shining streets and harbor waters. The thousands downtown who pressed against the taut ropes police and soldiers had stretched near the fire lines were impressed by a different view. To them the entire horizon seemed involved in an immeasurable sea of fire, smoke and steam.

Restaurants on the outskirts of the fire zone did a rushing business. A number of companies, such as Leonhardt's Wagon Company on Saratoga Street, kept open house all night, treating friends and customers to coffee, sandwiches and oysters on the half shell. Many spectators, pitying firemen who could not leave their posts, rushed home to make coffee and sandwiches for them. Some firemen were so busy with sudden outbreaks of new blazes that they kept both hands on the hoses while they were fed by Samaritans. One fireman, to show his appreciation for the lunch,

27

The Maryland Institute Building in "Marsh Market Space" burned for three-quarters of an hour before a stream of water was put on it. Only these jagged walls remain. The residences in the foreground (north of Baltimore Street) were spared.

took his donor's empty basket into a burning warehouse and filled it with walnuts, some already scorched.

The wet, grimy firemen, their eyes puffed up and inflamed from smoke, were not only hungry, they were also bone-tired. Those who could not be spared from their posts tied their hoses to boxes or to telephone poles while they rested in nearby doorways. Those who were granted rest periods staggered into nearby buildings to lie down on the floor or on desks. One told friends later that he was so tired that he slept on a counter for three hours. When he awakened, the fire, which had leapfrogged over his building, was six blocks away.

The fire at the Maryland Institute drove residents of Centre Market Space—then commonly called "Marsh Market"—some with screaming children in their grasp, to the east side of Jones Falls. As the building burned, the main body of the swirling flames hurried east toward it. The north side of Fayette Street was flaming as far as the west side of Gay Street, where the Church of the Messiah was ablaze. From that corner the fire veered south, lopping off a chunk of the southeast corner of Gay and Baltimore Streets, and then went east again on the south side of Baltimore to the Falls. It did not cross the Falls at this point, but, gathering momentum from the wind which was blowing at a rate of nearly thirty miles per hour, hurtled south through the financial district toward the five long piers, filled with combustibles, stretching off Pratt Street.

The speed and intensity of the fire were tremendous. Substantial buildings occupied by banks, investment houses and insurance companies fell as easily and quickly as though they were so much tinder. The Chamber of Commerce Building, the Stock Exchange and the Merchants Club were swept by flames. So great were the wind and the vacuum caused by the heat that the streams from the hoses were torn to fragments and could not reach even the second stories.

Many men were still busy rescuing every last object they could. Employees of some companies succeeded in hauling away all their office furniture. One insurance brokerage firm saved everything except the long counter across the front of the office—and the employees even tried to take that. Other companies were not so lucky. Unable to secure

29

wagons, their employees could only save what they could carry, a few files and perhaps a typewriter. Office workers, carried away by the excitement, risked serious injury or even death by dashing up burning stairways to second and third floors to recover the petty cash box. Men cried as they watched flames crash into banks containing their own or their firms' money. They thought all was lost. Several employees of the Merchants National Bank, on the southeast corner of Water and South Streets, waited on the steps until the flames approached. Before they were driven away they kissed the granite walls.

At 3:30 a.m. Mayor McLane told a *Sun* reporter, "I feel the conflagration shows some signs of abating." Police Marshal Farnan was more optimistic. He said, "I think the fire is practically under control."

Evidently neither one knew what was occurring on the south side of the fire. By 3 o'clock the southwest wing of the blaze which had encountered difficulty in pressing through the large buildings on the north side of Lombard Street, finally crossed Charles Street below Lombard. A magnificent defense was made at the intersection by twenty-five men, hardly out of their teens, from two Relay volunteer fire companies who used old-fashioned hand engines. Their fight was so spectacular that the hundreds watching cheered them again and again as they beat back the flames with their meager equipment. Many thought that the hard-working, grinning young men had won until they noticed wisps of smoke, and then gashes of yellow fire rise in some of the old buildings on the east side of Charles. The buildings crumbled in an incredibly short time. By 5 a.m. the blaze had worked south on Charles to Balderston Street, which divides the block between Lombard and Pratt. Here the fire was checked. But back farther the flames in the first block of West Lombard Street, fed by oils and chemicals stored in warehouses, had already moved south down the middle of that block to the rear of the Maltby Hotel and through it to Pratt Street.

By 4 a.m. the north side of Pratt, almost down to the Falls, was burning. Blazing turpentine and lumber sent up pillars of smoke that looked like gigantic exclamation marks until the wind dissipated them. A half hour later the powerhouse annex of the United Railway & Electric Company on the south side of Pratt between Frederick Street and Centre

30

Baltimore and South Streets looking southwest. The ruins of the fifty-four-year-old Sun Iron Building—the first iron structure in the city—are on the left. The famous five-story building, designed by the daring R. G. Hatfield, was the progenitor of the modern skyscrapers.

Market Space went down with a crash. Its eleven engines, ranging from 250 to 3,500 horsepower, were buried in the wreckage. When they stopped the electric current went off. Streetcars that had still been running stopped abruptly, sometimes in the middle of blocks. Lights went out. Streets not illuminated by the flames were enveloped in gloom which was relieved only by the faint glow from gas and naphtha lamps.

Engine companies, both local and from out of town, were strung out along the south side of Pratt Street, pumping water from the harbor. They were aided by the *Cataract* which moved back and forth, pouring water where it seemed to be needed most. The wind, however, split the spray from the massed streams and made them ineffectual.

31

THE SUN

CXXXIV—NO. 84.　　　　BALTIMORE, MONDAY MORNING, FEBRUARY 8, 1904.　　　　PRICE ONE CENT

TWENTY-FOUR BLOCKS BURNED IN HEART OF BALTIMORE

CITY'S MOST VALUABLE BUILDINGS IN RUINS

LOSS ROUGHLY ESTIMATED AT FIFTY MILLION DOLLARS

Starting In John E. Hurst Building The Fire Sweeps South To Lombard, East To Holliday And North To Lexington, Destroying Wholesale Business Houses, Banks, Trust Buildings, B. And O. Central And Other Prominent Structures.

The Sun's Monday morning editions were printed in Washington and rushed back to Baltimore by train. Baltimoreans, avid for news of the fire, paid newsboys extravagant prices for them.

Shortly after midnight the vessels on the north side of the basin were getting ready to move. When the flames began to lap at Pratt Street all the ships and smaller craft seemed to move at once toward the lower harbor. There was such a sudden exodus of steamers, bay schooners, barges and tugs that collisions could be avoided only with difficulty. Some tugs from the lower harbor created additional confusion and jams by moving toward the Pratt Street docks to help with the rescue work. The tug *Oriole* pulled out barges all along the piers. Later in the day the *Oriole* pushed into Smith's dock at the foot of Gay Street when her captain, Vivian Phillips, heard cries of help. The flour mill of the C. A.

32

Gambrill Manufacturing Company was burning and its employees were hemmed in by the flames. The *Oriole* took them off and placed them beyond the fire zone. The unfinished tug *Neptune* was loaded with $15,000 worth of goods from an endangered supply house and towed out to the harbor. Later in the morning the *Windom*, a Government steamer used as a revenue cutter, arrived from Annapolis under full steam. She helped fight the fire along the docks and then her officers and crew aided Baltimore and Ohio Railroad employees haul bags of coffee from a warehouse. They were stored on the decks of the *Windom* and the steamer *Potomac* until they could be moved back safely.

The morning editions of *The Sun* and the *Herald,* considering the circumstances, contained vivid accounts of the fire. The *Herald* used eight-column streamers acrosss its front page (all, incidentally, written by Mencken). They read:

HEART OF BALTIMORE WRECKED

BY GREATEST FIRE IN CITY'S HISTORY

A Thousand Buildings Burned: Loss Over $75,000,000

Dynamite Used To Combat Flames In Vain—

All Of Chief Skyscrapers Destroyed

Extra Engines Brought Here From All The Neighboring Cities

Entire District Between Howard And Gay And Fayette Street
And Pratt Street In Ruins

The main article of *The Sun,* which had been written in longhand on the bar of the Lexington Hotel by Frank R. Kent, began, "Fire which started at 10:50 o'clock yesterday morning, devastated practically the entire central business district of Baltimore and at midnight the flames were still raging with as much fury as at the beginning.

"To all appearances Baltimore's business section is doomed. Many of the principal ranking institutions, all the leading trust companies, all the largest wholesale houses, all the newspaper offices, many of the principal retail stores and thousands of smaller establishments went up in flames, and in most cases the contents were completely destroyed.

The Baltimore American Building, Baltimore and South Streets, was gutted late Sunday night. The famous newspaper was unable to publish its account of the fire until Tuesday. Note the unburned wooden pole in front of the fire-smashed stone walls.

"What the loss will be in dollars no man can even estimate, but the sum will be so gigantic that it is hard for the average man to grasp its magnitude. In addition to the pecuniary loss, will be the immense amount of business lost by the necessary interruption to business while the many firms whose places are destroyed are making arrangements for resuming business.

"There is little doubt that many men, formerly prosperous, will be ruined by the events of the last twenty-four hours. Many of them carry little or no insurance, and it is doubtful if many of the insurance companies will be able to pay their losses dollar for dollar, and those that do will probably require time in which to arrange for the payment."

34

Both *The Sun* and the *Herald* had been printed in Washington.*
The Sun had made arrangements early Sunday afternoon with the Washington *Evening Star* to print the next morning's *Sun* there if the Iron Building had to be abandoned. A B. & O. special train was engaged and it was standing by at Camden Station as early as 4 p.m. At 11 p.m. when the Iron Building appeared doomed, orders were given to *The Sun* men to proceed to Camden. In addition to an editorial crew the group consisted of the entire force of the composing room and mailing department and several clerks from the counting room. Between 3 and 4 a.m. *The Sun's* extra was on the press.

The *Herald* crew arrived in Washington around midnight. It consisted of Mencken, several members of his staff, fifteen or twenty printers and small squads of pressmen and circulation hustlers. Outside the B. & O. station in Washington the men paused to look back at the red glow over Baltimore. The four-page *Herald* was printed by the Washington *Post* after that paper had gone to press.

The *Herald* crew was back in Baltimore with 20,000 papers, brought over in a baggage car, by 8:45 a.m. *The Sun* had its papers in downtown Baltimore before 5 a.m., beating its rival on the big story by about four hours. Although both papers normally sold for a penny, Monday morning in the downtown area they brought as much as 25 cents.

Long before daylight, while the fire was spreading through the financial district, there was panic in East Baltimore. The scene in the general area from Caroline Street to Broadway and Eastern Avenue to the waterfront was described by observers as "heart-rending." Many residents had piled their household goods on the sidewalks or were wildly throwing bedding, clothing and furniture out of upstairs windows. At one corner in Little Italy hurdy-gurdies and orchestrions were lined up, like hacks at a downtown intersection. Children, parents and old folks were in tears. Many did not know what to do. Others, with bundles under their arms or packs on their backs, rushed for the Broadway ferry to cross over to

---

*The Baltimore *American* did not appear on Monday morning. It resumed publication on Tuesday from the building of Frank A. Munsey's Washington *Times* where its publication was continued until February 27. The Baltimore *Evening News* was printed at the office of the Washington *Post* from February 8 to the 22nd. *The Sun* was printed in Washington until April 6. The February 9th issue of the *Herald* was printed at the plant of the Baltimore *World*, which was outside of the burnt district. On February 10 the *Herald* again made use of facilities in Washington. For the next five weeks it was printed by the Philadelphia *Evening Telegraph*.

Looking south from the roof of the Calvert Building. The Maryland Trust Company Building is on the left. Before the fire, Light Street, on the right, was only between forty-one and forty-five feet wide. It was widened to nearly 110 feet between Baltimore and Pratt Streets. The section beyond the fire area, between Pratt and Lee Streets, eventually was widened to 126 feet.

Locust Point. But attendants were forced to turn most of them away. The rush to the east was so great that the sidewalks were jammed and the people spilled out into the streets among the speeding wagons. Merchants along Broadway removed all their goods, storing them on sidewalks or in the streets, until they could be carted away. Wagons were again in great demand and the teamsters had raised their prices overnight. Everywhere there were tears, screams and the babble of voices—in the houses, in the stores, even in St. Leo's Catholic Church where residents of Little Italy cried appeals to their St. Anthony for deliverance from the flames.

After moving down the north side of Pratt Street to the Falls, one tip of the fire, turned by some strange quirk of the wind, skipped back along the south side of Pratt almost to Cheapside. At the same time the main blaze attacked buildings along the west side of the Falls.

36

Looking southwest from the Calvert Building. The International Trust Company on Baltimore Street is in the foreground. The street to the right of it is Charles. The building with the water towers on the far right is the Sutton Building, on the southeast corner of Liberty and Lombard Streets. The streets—but not the sidewalks—are cleared. Wisps of smoke still rise from the rubble.

The fighters' strategy was designed to keep the fire from jumping the seventy-five-foot-wide Jones Falls. Everyone from the district fire engineers to the county volunteers felt that if the fire got across on a large front while the strong winds continued from the northwest, East Baltimore would be doomed.

Thirty-seven engines were ordered to the main battle line—the last line of defense, as some called it—which coincided with the course of the Falls from Baltimore Street to the Block Street drawbridge. The bridges spanning the stream at every street were vantage points for the fire engines, many of which sucked water out of the Falls. The fight was so determined that one engine company refused to get off the burning Lombard Street bridge until that seemed ready to collapse. Engines that could not find room on the bridges lined up along East Falls Avenue. Firemen carried the hoses across in rowboats.

Late in the morning flames gutted practically every building along West Falls Avenue from Baltimore Street to the tip of Union Dock while blazing piles of lumber that edged the west side of the Falls threatened momentarily to ignite other stacks on the east side. From Pratt Street down flames ate into the warehouse of the T. J. Myer Packing Company, the building of the Boyer Fruit Packing Company, running back to Union Dock, and the Maryland Ice Company plant, a frame building connected by a large open shed with the Union Dock depot of the American Ice Company. Packing houses, wood and lumber yards on Union Dock caught fire. Streams from the *Cataract* managed to beat back the flames on some sections of the dock, but sparks and brands, between 11 a.m. and 1 p.m., flew across the Falls.

Some brands started several large fires there. Firemen groaned. But they kept fighting because they knew the fate of East Baltimore was involved. When one blaze jumped into a large lumber yard a fire chief said, "If this goes, she'll burn clean through to the country."

One of the first blazes on the east side was in some lumber piled next to Warehouse B of the Broadbent & Davis Mantel Company, at Canton Avenue and President Street. A fire company was ordered off the Canton Avenue bridge to fight it. The fire smouldered for several hours but finally was extinguished. The roof of Otto Duker's box factory, a short block to the east and north, caught fire, but the building was saved.

The worst fires occurred in the vicinity of Philpot and Thames Streets. The fertilizer works of Isaac Robinson & Company and the L. Sonneborn & Son Chemical Company were gutted. But two fire companies from Washington and Nos. 11, 18 and 15 of Baltimore rushed down from President Street to keep the fire from those two buildings, and the Maine Lake Ice Company, from spreading too far through the Shryock Lumber Company. By extraordinary effort the firemen saved the Shryock barn containing 5,000,000 feet of lumber.

Then the firemen won another battle. The malt house of Francis Denmead, across the street from the City Morgue at the foot of President Street, caught fire twice. Twice firemen put the flames out before they could spread to the surrounding large buildings and from there to the Canton waterfront. The fire on the east side of the Falls was under con-

A Naval Reservist has only devastation to guard on Pratt Street at Dugan's Wharf. Note the pile of hoops. The barrels and their contents were destroyed early Monday when the flames whirled crazily along narrow Pratt Street to Jones Falls.

trol. The only danger that remained was on the Savannah pier of the Merchants & Miners' Transportation Company off West Falls Avenue and Block Street.

Three times that afternoon lumber piled on the pier burst into flames. On the first occasion a steam launch rigged with a large wooden bucket put out the blaze by dumping water on it. Then two M. & M. tugs, the *Venus* and the *Mary*, were given hoses of a New York fire company and No. 11 of Baltimore which came rushing down from the malt house blaze. The tugs carried the nozzles as near as they dared to the dock while the engine companies pumped water from the Falls. The *Cataract* came along to help out. The combined force of water, aided by the wind which had switched to the north, pushed the fire back into territory already devastated and checked the forward march of the flames. East Baltimore was safe. The great fire was nearly out.

39

Long after the fire had roared to the east, firemen still work on a stubborn blaze in the B. & O. Building. Both it and the Equitable Building, right, were swept clean by the surging flames. The B. & O. Building was replaced by the Emerson Hotel.

There was not much left to burn in the immediate area west of the Falls and south of Baltimore Street. Gutted buildings crumbled and smoked but no great flames arose from them. The American Ice Company storage shed on West Falls Avenue was the last of 1,526 buildings to burn. It was filled with Kennebec ice and so fierce were the flames fed by the wooden walls and the sawdust preservative that the long cakes of ice almost seemed to burn too.

The great fire—one of the greatest in the history of American cities—was out.

Evidently no one recorded the precise time when the flames died down among the melting ice of the devastated storage shed. In fact, no one seemed to know exactly at what time the fire was considered out. The official report of the Fire Department declared that the "conflagration raged until 11:30 a.m. Monday." The report must have referred to the time when the fire *seemed* to be losing its force. The blaze was still great at a number of points until 2:30 p.m. The *Herald* said "it was all over —the great fire was out" between 2 and 3 o'clock. *The Sun* declared that "after 30 hours of defiance of all human agencies . . . the fire was officially declared under control at 5 p.m." Long after that, small islands of fire in the desolated areas—one of them was in the ruins of the Hurst Building where the conflagration started—would flare up suddenly, but they could not do any additional damage or threaten untouched property.

The fire had been fought by 1,231 firemen (plus about 400 unattached volunteers), fifty-seven engines, nine hook and ladder trucks, two hose companies, one fireboat, one revenue cutter, one police boat and many tugs. Of this number Baltimore itself furnished 460 firemen, twenty-four steam engines, eight hook and ladder trucks and numerous boats. The other men and equipment came from New York, Philadelphia, Washington, Wilmington, Chester, York, Altoona, Harrisburg, and Phoenixville, Pa., Annapolis, Sparrows Point, Relay and St. Denis. Atlantic City, N. J., furnished men, but no equipment. Some of the companies did not arrive until the second day of the fire. One of the last to show up was the New York detachment of 130 men with seven engines and seven hose carriages, accompanied by nineteen New York newspaper artists and reporters. It had been delayed by a combination of circumstances. The

Because a large quantity of gunpowder was stored in the hardware store of Anderson & Ireland, 42-44 East Pratt Street, firemen poured six streams of water on the building from 5 a.m. to 4 p.m. Monday. The water-soaked building became faced with ice.

first appeals to New York had been made by a group of Baltimore citizens. New York authorities replied that they could do nothing until an official request was made. By the time the formal appeal of the City of Baltimore had been received in New York it was late Sunday night. The special train carrying the detachment jumped the track at North Philadelphia, causing a long delay.

The railroad, in the haste of getting the special train together, coupled flat cars for the fire equipment between the day coaches for the firemen, severing the steamlines from the engine. As a result the coaches were without heat. No one had brought along any food. When the firemen arrived at the President Street Station they were disgusted, cold and hungry. But they were still willing to fight. Three of the companies were assigned to the vicinity of the station where sparks were setting off small fires. The others were dispatched along the Falls and to the docks. As they proceeded to their positions the men were welcomed with cheers and the waving of flags and tablecloths. After the New Yorkers had battled the flames for several hours they were sent in relays to a bay steamer moored off Light Street where they had a combination breakfast and dinner. The steamship company refused to take any money. So did a blacksmith who welded a broken axle on one of the engines.

The Baltimore Fire Department lost one steam engine, one hook and ladder truck and 29,900 feet—nearly six miles—of hose. The total amount of hose in use was more than 91,000 feet. Officials estimated that the fire was doused with 70,000,000 gallons of water. There never was any scarcity although there were many rumors during the fire that "the water supply had given out." A water engineer said later, "if there had been nozzles enough . . . we could have flooded the burning district." He also pointed out that while the greatest volume of water was being used, the water in the reservoir in service at that time actually rose 2/10 of an inch. The supply from the Gunpowder River was flowing in faster than the engines could pump it out.

Authorities discovered that there were no serious injuries and only one reported fatality. From Sunday morning to Monday afternoon firemen almost continuously risked their lives but not one was killed by the ripping flames or the many toppling walls. Their most serious injuries were second and third degree burns. Not one fireman, and only one policeman, had a bone broken. Police Capt. A. J. Pumphrey, while leading a detachment of 150 Philadelphia policemen down Baltimore Street, stumbled on a curbstone and fractured his ankle. The man reported dead —a lumber yard workman was said to have been driven by flames into the harbor where he drowned—may have been imaginary. There were conflicting reports on his name, age and address, and police never did recover the body.

There was no great rejoicing after the fire was out. People were too exhausted, physically and emotionally. And, even though the terrifying, consuming flames were gone, it was hard to be elated in the face of the appalling destruction.

An area of 140 acres—more than seventy blocks—had been burned out. By Fire Department count, 1,526 buildings and four large lumber yards were destroyed. The number of business enterprises burned out—banks, manufacturers, merchants, etc.—totalled over 2,500.

Thousands of mechanics, clerks, bookkeepers, stenographers, salesmen and laborers were out of work because their places of employment were in ruins. The State Labor Bureau estimated the number of those temporarily jobless at about 35,000.

Streets were choked with half-burnt brick, crumpled sheets of tin, broken glass, charred timbers, tangled masses of wire and the splintered stumps of electric poles. At Baltimore and Light the only thing in a perpendicular position was the framework of a large iron street clock. Buildings made of stone, iron and concrete were in ruins. The skyscrapers were shattered shells streaked with black fire marks. Even businessmen who knew the downtown section well had difficulty in determining where certain streets lay under the ruins, heaped many feet high. The mass of people—including many sightseers from out-of-town—saw a monotony of destruction that was relieved only by the figures of a few workmen or firemen slowly and cautiously making their way over the ruins.

A *Sun* reporter, one of the few observers allowed inside the burnt district, wrote these impressions, "Walking through the streets, within the lines drawn by the militia, the grim ruins of fine buildings that forty hours ago towered high in the air confront the spectator at every turn. Great financial institutions, banks and business houses that for years have reared their stately heads skyward are now leveled to earth, until in some cases hardly one brick remains upon the other, and the wreckage is scattered broadcast, so that streets and sidewalks are concealed alike. Here and there the hollow shell of some tall structure stands straight and grim, blackened and denuded from roof to cellar, a monument to the fiery hurricane that swept through the city. Throughout the burned district there existed . . . an almost complete and terrifying silence that added to the grimness of the spectacle and caused a feeling of awe among the few who were allowed to go within the lines . . . Those who wandered about the scenes where the fire had done its work of destruction were chary of disturbing the silence and none could look upon the wreck of so

44

Smoke still rises from the rubble while workmen clear debris from the street, and businessmen, who needed permits to enter the burnt area, inspect what little is left of their smoldering buildings which lie in absolute ruin.

much that was fine and magnificent in the city without feelings of the most intense sorrow and sadness."

Thousands clamored to get inside the burnt district but they were turned back by the soldiers, no matter how urgent the plea, unless they had a military pass which ordered the "officers of the guards at all points to pass bearer at all hours." The passes were issued at police and military headquarters in the Court House, and all day long the corridors of the building were lined with hundreds of applicants. Men wanted to go into the burnt area to check safes, to take pictures, to make sketches, or just to look around. Most were turned down because authorities felt that lives would be endangered by the smouldering fires and tottering walls. The majority of those who got passes were bankers who were anxious to

Several desks and a chair, rescued at the last minute from a burning building, still stand in the middle of Baltimore and Liberty Streets. Mangled fire hose can be seen among the rubble.

inspect the conditions of the vaults containing stocks, bonds (many not registered), valuable papers, notes and millions in currency.

All of Baltimore was worried about the contents of the vaults. Anxious depositors and boxholders appeared along the roped-off streets early in the morning to find out if their valuables were safe. In the crowd were millionaires, merchants, tradesmen, and many women. Not infrequently a woman would be crying and wringing her hands with anxiety as she asked one passerby after another about the condition of a deposit vault. Not even the bankers knew for sure. They thought that the contents were safe, but they had been advised by experts not to open the vaults until they had cooled. When one red-hot safe was opened by its impatient owner every piece of paper in it immediately burst into flames. The documents had survived until then for the simple reason that, despite the terrific heat, there was not oxygen enough in the hermetically sealed safe to cause combustion. But when the safe was opened, the outside air rushing in provided the oxygen and the papers ignited instantly.

The condition of the vaults was not the only concern. Authorities also were troubled by the amount of drinking, the possibility of looting, and the weakened walls and buildings.

Marshal Farnan, after a conference with Mayor McLane, Judges Harlan and Stockbridge, ordered all saloons closed until further notice. The original order by Police Commissioner Upshur Sunday morning banning the sale of liquor evidently was never transmitted to Farnan during the excitement. In announcing the new edict, Farnan said, "There has been too much drunkenness, and there shall be no more. Drunken men only give the police trouble and are liable to do more harm to themselves than anyone else." By noon police had arrested 150 intoxicated men. Every case was dismissed by the magistrates.

Two men were charged with larceny of several bundles of cigars "from persons unknown." Sneak thieves and pickpockets—a number from out of town—were picked out of the crowds by detectives from Baltimore and other cities and locked up. *The Sun* noted that all necessary precautions had been taken "to prevent looting [which occurs] when some dire calamity causes the human birds of prey to flock to the scene for purposes of pillage and, perhaps, even murder. Owing undoubtedly to the prompt and effective measures taken, Baltimore has been singularly free from this gruesome addition to her other calamities."

Early on the second morning the mayor, after conferring with Francis N. Jencks and Theodore Marburg, decided to call upon the U. S. Government for help. Jencks and Marburg went to Washington to see Secretary of War Taft with a request that he send a corps of "experienced" engineers to Baltimore immediately to do additional dynamiting. At that hour the fire was moving eastward and, in the opinion of officials, the only salvation of the section seemed to be to demolish a large area ahead of the flames. The Secretary of War ordered sixty Army engineers dispatched at once and they arrived in Baltimore around 3 p.m. By that time the flames were dying down. Authorities then asked the engineers to demolish dangerous walls in the burnt district. The major in charge of the detachment inspected some of the leaning walls and gutted buildings. He told the mayor he was opposed to blowing them up because he believed the charges would endanger lives and property. He suggested instead the use of grappling hooks. And he intimated that they could be used just as well by the city's clean-up force. Before 6 p.m. he and his men returned to Washington.

Building Inspector Preston had been so confident that the engineers would do the demolition work that he sent out six squads to chalk-mark each wall and building that should be knocked down.

On their tour the inspectors discovered that several buildings which had been in the midst of the hottest infernos suffered only slight damage. The one-story Alexander Brown & Sons Building, on the southwest corner of Baltimore and Calvert Streets, had its windows broken and its outside walls fire marked, but otherwise it was not damaged. Firemen thought that the tremendous updraft created by the flames at the B. & O. and Continental Buildings saved it. At the Safe Deposit & Trust Company Building, on South Street between the gutted Iron Building and the ruined structure of the Commercial and Farmers National Bank, the only interior damage was a partially burned desk in the president's office.

Another establishment that escaped was J. G. Pertsch's lunchroom on East Fayette Street. The fire was stopped next door in a saloon whose free lunches must have hurt the lunchroom's business. Pertsch helped firemen who were trying to get their hoses into the saloon by throwing brick after brick through its windows.

A West Lombard Street saloonkeeper had better luck, but he did not realize it immediately. Sunday afternoon he thought his place was in the path of the fire so he moved everything but the bar itself to a warehouse on Concord Street, then many blocks from the fire. The saloon never burned but the warehouse—and the transferred goods—were a total loss. The saloonkeeper was an unhappy man until he learned that his insurance would cover the destroyed property even though it had been moved from a building that did not burn to one that did.

The most popular stories, the ones told over and over again by the crowds roaming the streets, were the wind and umbrella tales. The

48

tremendous draft of the fire had shot papers and pieces of wood high into the air and the strong winds had carried them remarkable distances. Pieces of books, accounting sheets, telegrams, letters, even paper money, were blown all over northeast Baltimore and far out into the counties. One man exhibited the charred corner of a check drawn on the National Mechanics Bank he found in Baltimore Cemetery, about two miles from the blaze. Another carried around a half-pound piece of wood he found on Broadway near McElderry Street. A boy showed part of a torn $10 bill he picked up far beyond the city limits. Some of the stories must have been exaggerated. One spectator told of seeing a large heavy ledger book flying far beyond the fire zone. Others reported burning brooms, fiery timbers "the size of a man" and the wooden cornices of buildings high in the sky. An Eastern Shoreman exhibited a fragment of a bill of lading of the Baltimore Steam Packet Company he said he picked up one and a half miles south of Rock Hall—across the Chesapeake Bay and about twenty-five miles from Baltimore.

The umbrella stories usually concerned distinguished citizens who were out Sunday afternoon with their umbrellas open. When flying sparks struck, the cloth would disintegrate. Many of the umbrella holders, so the stories went, were carrying only the bare ribs above their heads, happily ignorant that the covering was gone and that their hats were smoking.

By 4 p.m.—while firemen still were fighting flames along the west side of the Falls and on the docks—workmen were busy at the new United Railway & Electric Company's power station. This one, in contrast to the old building adjoining it, was only slightly damaged. After linemen had strung new wires on it, the engineers were ready to turn on the four 4,000-horsepower engines. The downtown section again had electricity. As soon as there was power, streetcars began to move. Motormen and conductors had stayed in the cars during the 11-hour stoppage. In many cases their wives and children, who brought them food, stayed with them. During the tieup Baltimoreans either walked or paid fancy prices to ride in wagons and carts.

The resumption of streetcar service did much to cheer the citizens Thousands more poured into the downtown section in the evening to

49

The fire swept through the financial district like a fiery hurricane, leaving in its wake only gaunt skeletons of walls and millions of broken, scorched bricks. This was the view at South and Lombard Streets after the fire had rushed east.

view the ruins. Restaurants were crowded. Some, because of a shortage of food, served only coffee and sandwiches. Ford's Opera House and the Academy of Music postponed scheduled performances until Tuesday night, but two other theaters opened. The Maryland Theater presented "A Pair of Pinks," and the Chase, featuring the George Fawcett stock company, "The Two Orphans." Both were well attended and the audiences enjoyed the plays.

The municipal departments in the City Hall were open all day, but little work was done except in the mayor's office where numerous conferences were held concerning the fire and public safety. Some bankers called on the mayor to object to the blasting of damaged buildings because the concussions might damage safes and vaults. The Citizens Permanent Relief Committee met with the mayor to consider means of relieving distress. He revealed that there was only about $10,000 in the city's contingent fund. At a conference attended by the mayor, the governor, the attorney general and the city solicitor, it was decided to ask the Legislature to authorize a city loan of $2,000,000. The City Council met and adjourned until February 19. Messages of sympathy and offers of help came from across the nation. The one from Boston read, "All our people profoundly sympathetic with Baltimore in its woeful affliction and proffer their aid and services in any way needed." The mayor of Macon, Ga., telegraphed, "The City of Macon extends sympathy. Would that we were nearer to render substantial aid." Chicago, Albany, N. Y., and many other far distant cities, offered to send fire companies and men. Their offers were declined with thanks.

In Washington Congressman Emrich, representing Illinois but a native Baltimorean, introduced a bill in the House to appropriate $1,000,000 for the relief of Baltimore. Part of the bill read, "The fire has so crippled the merchants and business interests in the city of Baltimore that they are unable to adequately and properly provide and care for the many who are rendered homeless and penniless by the disaster." Congressman Emrich evidently did not know that only a very few were made homeless. The bill was referred to the Committee of Appropriations and eventually died there.

The Maryland Legislature, meeting Monday night in Annapolis, under a suspension of the rules, passed a law that the days from February 8th to the 15th inclusive should be legal holidays and "as regards the presenting for payment or acceptance, and the protesting of notes, drafts and bills shall be treated as Sunday."

BEFORE — In 1903 the Baltimore skyline looked like this

|←————————— FROM WEST TO EAST—13 BLOCKS OF RUIN—→|

AFTER — A view from the same spot — after the Great Fire

A panorama of the Port of Baltimore made in 1903 from Federal Hill. J. William Schaefer, a Baltimore photographer who constructed the first panoramic camera to stop motion, took this picture. Light Street is on the left, Long Dock on right. Note the buildings on the wharves.

Mr. Schaefer made this photograph from the same spot while the smoke was still rising from the ashes of a fire-swept city. The harbor front is in complete ruins. The large, so-called fire-proof buildings at the left center are gutted. Over 1,500 buildings were destroyed in the fire.

53

*On Monday thousands of sightseers—many from nearby towns—crowded the downtown section
to stare at the ruins. They were kept beyond the burnt district by rope barricades and armed
guardsmen. Note the stone walkways across the cobblestone streets.*

54

And in the days that followed

RE-BIRTH

EARLY TUESDAY, while fires still smouldered in crumbling buildings and among bales of cotton on Union Dock, Baltimore rolled up its sleeves and went to work.

The city of 539,000 inhabitants, confronted by acres and acres of ruins, was not panic-stricken or even overwhelmed. The first numbing reaction of utter hopelessness was gone—displaced by a surge of confidence. The question no longer was, "How will we live?" but "What's to stop us from building a better city?" Somehow—without a leader, without a plan —Baltimore took heart.

Looking back fifty years it is difficult to determine what intangible force drove the people on in the face of disaster and ruin. It could have been any of a great many things. But, most likely, it was something compounded of faith, resolution and spirit—the same kind of spirit that fired the Baltimoreans of another century to beat back the British at North Point and Fort McHenry.

Whatever it was—heart or faith—the people needed a lot of it.

A visitor, after viewing the devastation, remarked, "It was as though the wrath of God descended while His eyes were closed."

Twenty banks were smashed and gutted. The condition of their vaults, containing millions in currency and millions more in securities, was still uncertain. Large portions of the wholesale, jobbing and produce districts were wiped out. The clothing manufacturing center was burned over. Wharf property from Light Street to Jones Falls was wrecked. Eight hotels, nine newspaper plants and nine transportation offices, including

55

The heart of a city in ruins—This view, from Charles and Lombard Streets, shows most of the 140 acres devastated by the two-day fire. To the right of O'Neill's (A) is the Union Trust Building (B). The next large structure is the Herald Building (C), then the Court

the headquarters of the B. & O., had been destroyed. The largest office buildings, while still standing, were hollow shells. All but two insurance offices were wrecked and many of their records burned. There was much doubt whether insurance companies could cover even half the losses. The future was as dim as the haze which hung over the burnt area.

Nevertheless, Tuesday's newspapers were crowded with advertisements which told a story of determination. Wise Brothers Company stated, "Everything running as usual. Employees report as early as convenient." The B. & O., although badly crippled by the destruction of its main offices, was ready for business. In a front page ad it told employees what to do, "Motive power employees report to the Mount Clare shop. Accounting department forces report to the Heywood Building, Pratt and Greene Streets. Engineering forces report to Mount Royal Station. All other forces report to Camden Station." Alexander Brown & Sons, with debris piled up all around it, announced that its building was so slightly damaged that it was ready for business as soon as the streets

56

House (D), the Calvert Building (E) (just in front of it is the C. & P. Telephone Building), the Equitable Building (F), the B. & O. main offices (G), City Hall (H), the Maryland Trust Building (I) and behind it the Continental Building.

could be cleared. The George A. Fuller Company, a construction firm, used the largest ad in *The Sun* to say it was prepared "to immediately commence the construction of buildings in Baltimore in place of those destroyed by fire."

The mood of the city was reflected in *The Sun's* editorial, which read in part, "It is the duty of every Baltimorean, as it should be his pleasure, to devote his energies to the task of making Baltimore a greater city than it was even before this colossal disaster. It can be done and it should be done without delay . . . Baltimore has an opportunity now to show the world that it possesses as much vitality—as much resource and strength— as any commercial, industrial and financial city in the United States. That its merchants, financiers and businessmen generally will prove themselves superior to any stroke of ill fortune, however grievous, is the belief of everybody who knows the spirit which animates them."

The first big job was finding temporary quarters for the thousands of companies and individuals who had been burned out.

57

Workmen remove debris from around The Savings Bank of Baltimore, Gay and Water Streets. The bank was permitted to open temporary offices in the Court House because of its large number of depositors, aggregating about twelve and a half per cent of the population.

On the recommendation of the Supreme Bench of Baltimore, Mayor McLane authorized The Savings Bank of Baltimore to use the license rooms of the Court of Common Pleas. The bank was given preferential treatment "in view of the large number of depositors, aggregating approximately twelve and a half per cent of the population." Many companies opened offices in the Rennert and Stafford hotels for a few days until they found larger temporary quarters. There was such a scramble for office and store space that businessmen took anything available. After meeting for a short time at the Stafford, the Stock Exchange moved to the Academy of Fine Arts. The American Bonding Company opened offices in a Negro school at Saratoga and Courtland Streets. The local office of the Standard Oil Company rented the stately Greenway mansion on the northwest corner of Mount Vernon and Washington Places, where the Washington Apartments now stand. A wholesale grocer took over a Negro Baptist church on Howard Street. John E. Hurst Company used the Fifth Regiment Armory. Other firms rented space in private homes, boarding houses, livery stables and even in dilapidated buildings. The German Fire Insurance Company moved into a deserted ruin which stood where the Municipal Building now is, and built temporary quarters on the first floor even before getting permission of the owners, who were unavailable at the time.

The demand for space was so great that property owners could charge exorbitant rents. Three small empty rooms on Liberty Street that had rented for $40 a month went for $200. The first floor of a Liberty Street home brought $75—$35 more than the rent of the entire house. A bonding company reputedly paid $6,000 to rent part of a church. Another company was considering a storeroom under the Central Y.M.C.A. building at $10,000 a year; the B. & O., anxious to get that place for a freight office, gladly paid $15,000.

The experiences of Turner & Thomas, an insurance agency that was burned out of its offices on Commerce Street, were typical of many firms. On Tuesday the agency opened temporary offices on North Calvert Street in an unfinished attic. Secondhand kitchen chairs and tables substituted for office furniture. Heat was furnished by two egg stoves. In the excitement on Sunday, employees had forgotten to save such office necessities as pencils, pens and writing paper. On Tuesday the staff had nothing to write with or on. Most of the downtown stationery stores were burned out or their supplies were exhausted—everyone needed pens and paper. F. Albert Roloson, a young insurance clerk at the time, finally got writing material at a neighborhood store that specialized in school supplies.

The important records of Turner & Thomas had been removed from the old office on Sunday and sent to a storage warehouse in the 1100 block of Park Avenue. In its new office the agency had no place to safeguard them overnight. It solved the problem by making arrangements

59

The United States Fidelity and Guaranty Company and the First National Bank established temporary offices in this former church on Saratoga Street near Cathedral. Other companies had offices in homes, boarding houses and school buildings.

60

with a catering firm. Every morning a wagon picked up the records at the warehouse and delivered them to the Turner & Thomas office. At 5 p.m. the catering firm sent a wagon to return the records to the warehouse. The shuttle service continued for two months—until the agency got a safe. Before one could be installed a building inspector had to examine the attic floor to determine what size safe it could support. When the agency asked the storage company for its bill, it received a statement with this notation scrawled across it, "*Charges—nothing but good will.*" The driver of the wagon who had hauled the agency's records also was instructed to return the large tip given him.

In addition to office space, businessmen from the burnt district had two other immediate problems—checking on their insurance claims and getting passes to go inside the damaged area.

On Tuesday all passes in circulation were summarily revoked. The mayor announced that new passes would go only to those "whose work necessitates their presence within the lines." Passes were confined to groups working under the City Engineer, employees of the Street Cleaning Department who were removing debris, crews from the Water Department who were repairing mains, and men under the building inspector who were tearing down weak walls and damaged buildings.

In explaining the action the mayor said, "I appreciate the fact that there are bank presidents, heads of financial institutions and many others with tremendous interests in the burned district who are anxious to see whether the valuables in safes and vaults have been preserved and to secure them. After a time, and as soon as possible, they will be permitted to enter, a guard will be sent along with them, but just now I think a little understanding will show what we have done is the only safe thing to do and will act for the general good."

On Tuesday the insurance men formed the General Loss Committee under the chairmanship of Paul Turner. One of his first acts was to insert this ad in the newspapers, "To the sufferers by loss in the Great Fire— To expedite matters, the insurance companies have appointed a General Loss Committee with headquarters at the Royal Arcanum building opposite the Hotel Rennert. All inquiries will be answered and any courtesy extended or advice given absolutely free of charge as to the procedure concerning adjustments. All persons are advised to make out complete lists of their insurance, giving names of companies and amount carried by it, and present it to headquarters either direct or through their agents or brokers, so that the proper committee may be assigned."

Turner was an excellent administrator. By Wednesday he had a complicated procedure worked out, the office open, and fifteen clerks on duty to process the claims, most of which involved a number of companies.

Small claims—the average policy did not exceed $2,500—were settled directly by individual companies. The first claims were paid on Wednesday. The first was for $300, the second $1,000.

The most important record each insurance company possessed was the "block book," which listed the property insured by the company in each block. With the book, the company could figure its total liability for the fire, and, consequently, determine if it were still solvent. Soon after the fire, Amherst B. Hall of the Baltimore Equitable Society hurried through the burnt district with his book, checking off the losses the Society had incurred. When he got to the last page he estimated that his company's losses would not exceed $2,000,000. His rapid calculations were amazingly close. The Society paid out about $1,900,000. And it had more than $400,000 remaining in its surplus funds, so it was still solvent.

A misplaced block book caused anxiety among officials of the German Fire Insurance Company for a week. On Sunday while clerks were stuffing everything they could get into the vault, the secretary of the company put the book on his desk so he would not forget to take it with him. When he left the room for a moment, someone else, not realizing what it was, threw it into the crowded vault. Not until the vault was opened six days later did the nervous official find the book and then learn that the company's total liability would not exceed its surplus.

For six days after the fire Baltimore lived in a constant and feverish state of excitement, bustle and confusion.

Here are just a few of the other things that happened:

The North German Lloyd steamer *Willehad,* which had been refused permission by immigration authorities to dock on Monday, finally disembarked 470 passengers on Tuesday. Many were German immigrants whose first view of the bright new world was one of ruins such as they had never seen in their battered old world. Some wanted to go back immediately.

While the immigrants sat mournfully and apprehensively in quarantine, the people of East Baltimore, paying little attention to the still smoking ruins west of the Falls, were singing, dancing in the streets, and kissing one another on the doorsteps of their homes. East Baltimore was celebrating its good luck in being spared by the flames. All day, long lines of wagons moved possessions back from the Highlandtown Hills to Broadway, the Polish colony and "Little Italy."

During the afternoon a large group of officials, followed by guardsmen, police and reporters, stumbled through the ruins to the vault of the Hopkins Place Savings Bank—the first bank vault to be opened after the fire. Heat had expanded the door and it took the perspiring and nervous bankers more than an hour to pull it open. The contents—more than $6,000,000 in cash and securities—were safe. Word spread rapidly over Baltimore and everyone felt better.

A few hours later the mayor declared that the city was declining all offers of assistance. "I do not mean that we are too proud to ask for help," he said, "and if we find that we need it I shall not hesitate three minutes about availing ourselves of the many generous and hearty offers of assistance, both financial and otherwise, that have poured in upon us from all over the country."

Wednesday morning the Consolidated Gas Company suggested, "On account of water having gotten into some of the gas mains it is advisable not to leave lights burning in unoccupied or sleeping rooms." Businessmen suggested that the municipal government ask Washington for Federal troops to help guard the city. Everyone had a suggestion for rebuilding Baltimore. The ones made most frequently were to widen Fayette, Light and Charles Streets and to open Hanover Street, which then stopped at Baltimore Street, through to Fayette. Many had suggestions on how to prevent another conflagration. One of the most unusual came from a Washingtonian. "I would suggest that fireproof shields should be put on roofs," he wrote. "These should be long enough to reach the pavement and should be worked from there. I also think such a contrivance would protect glass from heat and heavy hail storms."

A large crowd, including children, watches workmen prepare to topple the six-story wall to the right of the steam engine which provides the power for the operation. The view is looking east on Baltimore Street from Liberty, about five days after the fire.

City officials received complaints—from Baltimore and other cities—that tramps were posing as fire victims and soliciting alms.

Police arrested several saloonkeepers, two brewery employees and the manager of the Rennert Hotel for violating the liquor embargo. One man, caught transporting three barrels of beer, pleaded that he was taking it to a wedding in New York. Police arrested him anyway. Post Office clerks subscribed $100 to purchase coffee and sandwiches for firemen, policemen and soldiers. The Lend-a-Hand Club announced that it was organizing a relief auxiliary for young girls thrown out of employment by the fire. A number of organizations, including the Arion Singing Society and the Maryland Society of the Sons of the American Revolution, canceled or postponed scheduled balls, fetes and Washington Day celebrations. A guardsman, who had set the date for his wedding months before, managed to get to the church at the proper time only because his commanding officer gave him an emergency pass.

On Wednesday afternoon a fire broke out at 704 Cathedral Street—

the Hurst residence. It was a chimney fire and was extinguished by firemen without difficulty—quite unlike the fire that broke out Sunday morning in the building on German Street which was also owned by the Hurst family.

On Thursday morning, 3,000 laborers reported to the Street Cleaning Commission. After receiving workmen's tickets they were divided into squads and marched into the burnt district to clear the streets. One of their most difficult tasks was removing the steel girders, crumpled and twisted like ribbons, that fell from the Carrollton Hotel Annex across Baltimore Street. These had to be cut into small strips. But by nightfall Baltimore Street was cleared of rubble and Pratt and Hanover Streets were made passable for wagons. No attempt was made to do more than remove debris from curb to curb.

Some women noticed that the men were handling the rough brick and splintered iron pipes with their bare hands. Several ladies' aid societies said they would knit gloves for the workmen.

Hundreds of workmen, mostly unskilled laborers, were coming to Baltimore to get work. Out-of-town architects and contractors opened offices in hotel rooms to bid on the many building projects that were being planned. At the suggestion of city officials, railroads canceled plans for having excursion trains bring in the curious from Washington, Philadelphia and New York who were anxious to view the ruins.

The War Department told the mayor that it would not send Federal troops to Baltimore because it did not feel that they were necessary. *The Sun* commented, "The refusal is not surprising when it is remembered that when troops from New York under General Cobin were ordered here two days ago they were told they were not needed."

On Friday the national banks opened in temporary locations, and the mayor appointed a citizens' emergency committee to consider problems involved in rebuilding the burnt district. The committee, with William Keyser as chairman, consisted of forty-seven prominent citizens. Its duties were purely advisory. When it organized on Saturday it formed sub-committees for financial information, street improvements, legislation, taxation and finances, height of buildings and building laws, relations of city to Federal government, and for considering suggestions.

After a conference with the Board of Public Safety, Building Inspector Preston and other officials, the mayor declared that no building permits would be issued until plans were made for realigning "certain thoroughfares whose crookedness and narrowness have long constituted a blemish as well as a serious drawback to the city's progress." Charles C. Phelps, of the Municipal Electric Commission, said that the city would not permit the erection of a single pole or the stringing of a single wire for any purpose except street railways within the burnt district.

On Saturday instructions were distributed for the redemption of burnt paper money. The Treasury said it would readily exchange currency which could be identified and which comprised at least three-fifths of the bill. Notes of less than that size could be redeemed only when accompanied by an affidavit that remaining parts were wholly destroyed. All burnt money had to be taken or sent to Washington for exchange. An official said that the best way to carry the mutilated money was upon cushions of raw cotton.

In the afternoon Miss Alice Roosevelt, daughter of President Theodore Roosevelt, arrived in Baltimore to view the ruins. She was met at the Court House by General Riggs, who graciously waived the rule which prohibited women from entering the burnt district but did restrict her open barouche to Fayette Street, the northern boundary of the fire. A friend said she got "a fairly good view" of the ruins.

The hectic week closed on a rising tide of optimism. Business sources estimated that more than half the firms burned out were carrying all employees on the payrolls, and said many of them paid employees on Saturday afternoon. Considering the circumstances, a large volume of business was done during the week. Many firms, even though their plants and offices had been destroyed, kept on taking orders from their traveling salesmen, confident of their ability to get back on their feet in time to fill the orders. *The Sun* noted, "Already the city is recovering from the paralyzing blow it received. To a great extent business has been resumed and except for a change of location a majority of the establishments devastated by the conflagration have reestablished themselves in a temporary way. The streetcar system is in full operation except in the burned district; telephone and telegraphic communication is on again

Fire destroyed the six-story building occupied by Guggenheimer, Weil & Company, but missed the large sign the printing and lithographic firm had posted on the south side of the structure. A picture of this building aflame is on Page 6.

and the excitement of the past few days has subsided."

All that Sunday demolition crews pulled down or blew up swaying walls and shattered buildings. Most of the work was done by five gangs of forty men each who placed cables around the walls and then tugged, in chain gang fashion, until the masonry crumbled. The highest and thickest walls were blown up with dynamite or gun cotton. Lafferty, who directed the disastrous dynamiting during the fire, had been called back by city officials to supervise the cleanup work after the army engineers had refused to do it. In one day his men, using small charges which were wrapped in clay, leveled fourteen structures, including the Keyser, Consolidated and Stock Exchange buildings.

Sunday night in the burnt district, particularly in the financial section, the debris was illuminated by tiny flames from the week-old fire.

No one worried much about the flames. Baltimore, after seven days of tension and hard work, was relaxing. It even felt like laughing. It laughed at the story of the Boston newspaper that had a front-page sketch the day after the fire of the Washington Monument surrounded by fire engines, all pumping furiously while flames poured from windows of the residences on Mount Vernon Place. The fire, of course, never got within five blocks of the monument. It laughed at the story of the woman who lost an umbrella in the fire. She had left it in a piano store that had only been partially damaged by the flames. When she returned for the umbrella the proprietor told her that it had been burned, along with a number of pianos. She was indignant. "Why didn't you save the umbrella?" she asked. "That was at least one thing you could have carried out." The city also enjoyed the signs that had been put up in the burnt district. More than anything else they showed that the people had retained their sense of humor. Some of them read: "Evicted Against Our Will," "It Got Too Hot for Us Here. Call and See Us at Lexington and Park Avenue." "What Happened to Jones? The Story Will Be Told at His Temporary Location, 520 East Lafayette Avenue."

Saloons and bars, which had been closed since February 8, were allowed to open on Monday, February 15, at 5 a.m. The public was warned by authorities, however, that unless "peace and order prevailed" the drinking places would be promptly closed again. At 6 p.m. on Feb-

68

February sunlight plays on an unbroken second-story window in a broken building on the northwest corner of Hanover and Lombard Streets. Lights and shadows on the massive ruin in the background give it a soaring, cathedral-like appearance.

ruary 23, the Board of Police Commissioners, "believing that the emergency no longer requires the services of a military force in preventing disorder," released the National Guard regiments from guard duty. There were cheers all along the lines as the men packed up to go home. Baltimore policemen, who had worked almost a twenty-four-hour day during the fire and immediately thereafter, were continued on a semi-emergency twelve-hour-a-day shift for several months. In its annual report to the Mayor, the Board of Police Commissioners concluded its account of the fire by stating, "Not a single case of plundering happened, no serious depredations or losses were reported, or a life lost, though danger seemed present at every turn for days."

The General Loss Committee completed its work the latter part of July. It had handled 3,778 claims and paid out $29,074,358.51. When it closed its books eleven claims, involving $147,500, were still pending.

Between 1,000 and 1,200 additional claims had been settled directly by individual insurance companies.

The total fire and insurance losses were never figured out with any accuracy. The Insurance Year Book of 1904 said the property losses were $50,000,000. Other insurance sources, and many businessmen, estimated the total loss at about $100,000,000. The Year Book declared that insurance claims amounted to $35,000,000. In view of the General Loss Committee settlements of about $29,000,000, the Year Book figure seems about $5,000,000 too high. As a result of the fire, five Baltimore stock insurance companies failed, paying only sixty-four cents on the dollar. They were: Baltimore Fire Insurance Company, The Firemen's Insurance Company of Baltimore, Home Fire Insurance Company of Baltimore, Old Town Fire Insurance Company and Peabody Fire Insurance Company of Baltimore.

The gigantic task of improving and rebuilding the burnt district took a number of years.

While a program of reconstruction was being planned, the city continued its policy of refusing to issue building permits for the burnt district. For a week or so businessmen were patient. By the end of February they were so insistent about getting started that the city, still stalling for time to get a basic program worked out, gave them permission to build—at their own risk. It was pointed out that the risk would be condemnation of the new structure if the building line were changed by the widening of a street. On March 1 a few of the more intrepid businessmen began building operations.

The Citizens' Emergency Committee, which had met daily since its formation on February 12, worked out a detailed plan for street, market and wharf improvements by February 22, when it adjourned *sine die*. To execute this plan the city obtained from the Maryland Assembly an act which gave the mayor power to appoint a bi-partisan commission of four citizens who, together with the mayor, were to constitute the Burnt District Commission. The commission was empowered to initiate legis-

70

lation for the suggested improvements and to carry out the work within what was legally established as the fire line—a line that extended considerably beyond the actual fire line.

The commission was appointed on March 11, and confirmed by the Second Branch City Council the same day. Its members, who took the oath of office on March 12, consisted of Sherlock Swann and Charles K. Lord, Democrats; Reuben Foster and John T. Graham, Republicans, with the mayor *ex-officio*. Swann was elected chairman and James R. Brewer, Jr., secretary. Swann received $4,000 annually, the other members $3,500. Because no other space was available meetings were held in the City Hall's janitor room.

As soon as the commission organized it adopted the recommendations of the Emergency Committee as its recommendations. "The reason for such haste," the commission reported, "was that the public mind might be at once set at rest regards the improvements contemplated. As the matter had already been thoroughly considered no further deliberation was thought necessary."

But there were further deliberations. "Numerous persons and delegations came before the commission in opposition to one improvement or another," the report continued, "some claiming that Charles Street ought not to be widened, especially north of Baltimore Street; others that 100 feet would be unnecessarily wide for Light Street; others that the Courthouse Plaza was a mistake, etc.; but the widening of Baltimore Street from Liberty Street to Jones Falls, aroused the greatest opposition, and, unfortunately, was finally defeated in the City Council.

"The changes made in the original ordinance beside these were few. The widening of German Street, between Hopkins Place and Liberty Street, was eliminated; the Courthouse Plaza was reduced from a 160-foot width to one of 120 feet, and the widening of Charles Street was stopped at Fayette Street, instead of halfway between Fayette Street and Lexington Street. The reason advanced by the principal opposition to certain of the improvements, especially to the widening of Baltimore Street, was that it would take such a great length of time to complete that incalculable harm to the business interests of the city would result, for it was freely predicted that all of the improvements contemplated

71

Maryland National Guardsmen from Annapolis eat lunch in front of their mess tents on Fayette Street west of Gay Street. About 2,000 soldiers were on guard duty in the burnt district from February 8 to February 23. Not one case of looting was reported by authorities.

would take from five to ten years to carry out and almost bankrupt the city. Fortunately, these pessimistic forebodings were not fulfilled, for the commission's work was completed on August 10, 1905, being one year and five months from the date of its appointment, and the net cost was about $5,600,000 (the widening of Light Street, from Pratt Street to Lee Street, was a subsequent matter not included in the original recommendations, the net cost of which was about $550,000).

"After the general scheme of improvement had been finally adopted, with only the changes just cited, there was a great sigh of relief, for it had looked at one time as if the whole matter might have to be abandoned on account of the vigorous opposition of certain members of the City Council to one or another of the improvements; in fact, the situation had become so acute and the very backbone of the whole matter been in such jeopardy that the outcome was hard to foretell. Repeated conferences were held and every means exhausted to get the ordinance through in its original form, but without success. Finally, in order to save it, the changes mentioned were acceded to, but Mayor McLane

72

flatly announced that if any others were made he would veto the whole matter and accept the resignations of the Burnt District Commission, who agreed with him that their existence was useless if nothing important was to be accomplished."

The ordinance was passed on April 12. The commission at last had authority to execute some of its plans for a greater Baltimore. (It could not rebuild the Pratt Street waterfront until the voters passed the $6,000,000 dock improvement loan.)

The commission immediately announced that it would establish the new building lines on the streets to be widened so rebuilding could start. Only two property owners were interested. Others held back because the question of street grading—which did not come under the jurisdiction of the commission—was not yet settled. Even if a property owner knew where his new building line would be, he still did not know on what level to build his ground floor.

Before the grading ordinance was passed, a tragic event occurred which necessitated a change in the commission. On May 30, Mayor McLane, who had been married only sixteen days, committed suicide. He was succeeded in office by E. Clay Timanus. At the same time John W. Snyder replaced Foster, who had resigned from the commission a few days earlier.

When the grading ordinance was passed on June 23 the last obstacle to a large scale building program was finally removed. Early in July 8,778 laborers—plus more than 1,000 teamsters—were at work in the burnt district. Nearly 700 of this number were at work in the Calvert, Equitable, Continental and Union Trust buildings. After a careful examination, engineers had found the structures of all the skyscrapers to be in good condition. Carpenters and bricklayers, who were paid $3 a day, were hard at work rebuilding the skeletonized structures.

By mid-August, 236 buildings were under construction. Fifty-six were completed and fifty-two were occupied. By February, 1905, over 200 new places were occupied and 170 more under construction. On the first anniversary of the fire The Sun declared, "Baltimore looks back today on a year of recovery from the greatest disaster in her history. The event is of the nature of a thanksgiving—silent and without pomp and display.

73

Looking north on Charles Street toward the Union Trust Company Building before its fire-weakened stone walls were stripped by order of city authorities. The group of workmen are preparing to level the four-story skeleton of an elevator shaft on the right.

There will be no parading and no fireworks. Profoundly, gratefully, reverently, the population here is observing one of the most remarkable rehabilitations of any city in the world's history."

When the Burnt District Commission finally finished its work twelve streets had been extended or widened, a plaza had been established on the west side of the Court House and the wharf space south of Pratt Street between Bowley's Wharf and West Falls Avenue had been rebuilt with modern docks and piers.

The streets widened or extended were: Hopkins Place widened from Baltimore to Lombard; Hanover Street extended from Baltimore to Fayette; Charles Street widened from Fayette to Lombard; Light Street

74

The gaunt Union Trust Company Building after its outside walls had been stripped. The ten-story structure still stands on the northeast corner of Charles and Fayette Streets. The five skyscrapers gutted by the fire were rebuilt within the year.

75

widened from Baltimore to Pratt; St. Paul Street widened from Fayette to Baltimore; Calvert Street widened from Fayette to Baltimore; Commerce Street widened from Exchange Place to Pratt; West Falls Avenue extended from Baltimore to Lombard; German Street widened from Hopkins Place to Light; Lombard Street widened from Charles to South and from Gay to Centre Market Space; and Pratt from Light to Jones Falls.

The territory bounded by Baltimore Street, West Falls Avenue, Lombard Street and Centre Market Space was condemned and laid out for public market purposes and improved at a cost of about $435,000.

The fire—first regarded as the greatest misfortune ever to strike Baltimore—really did more for the city than any other single act in its entire history. It is highly doubtful that Baltimore, on its own initiative, would ever have risen from its ancient thralldom to narrow streets, rotting wharves and antiquated buildings. It would have been difficult, if not impossible, to obtain the consent of the citizens to tearing out the very heart of Baltimore—no matter how splendid the plans for rebuilding might have been. But the obliging fire did it in one great swoop—making possible a new start for the twentieth century.

The Burnt District Commission realized the opportunity—and the danger—as soon as it was organized. It noted in its report, "It was, of course, possible to clear away the debris, rebuild the houses on the old lines and begin business again, but had this been done the loss would indeed have been irreparable; therefore, the first thought was not how to simply restore the city, but how to make a greater one. Many of the buildings used for warehouses and other business purposes were old residences converted to such uses, occupying a great amount of space, but not at all suited to the economical transaction of business.

"The streets were wide enough, no doubt, for all the demands of long ago, but year after year they had become more and more congested, until the time had arrived when it was a serious question with merchants and a real handicap to their competition with those of other cities, so great was the average cost of delayed shipments, owing to the constant blockades of traffic. The wharves were in even worse condition, many of the docks being nothing more than mudholes, and so narrow that no

have collected mementoes which will be exhibited in a museum they plan to establish in the old No. 6 Engine House on Gay Street. The relics include a steam gauge from Engine No. 15, one of the two pieces of equipment destroyed in the fire, a picture of Goliath, and a derby. Goliath was a fire horse which pulled a piece of equipment to safety before a wall fell and for this deed became the only horse ever retired from the Fire Department; others were either sold or transferred to the Department of Sanitation. The most unusual item is the derby. Harvey R. Baker was wearing it when he was watching firemen enter the John E. Hurst Building, where the fire started. Holes were burned and cut in it from sparks and flying glass. For more than thirty years, on every anniversary of the fire, Baker would don the hat for the benefit of newspaper photographers.

The fire has been a memorable event for a surprising number of Baltimoreans born before the turn of the century. The *Baltimore Sun Magazine* has a feature, "I Remember When . . .," a first-person account of some past event, place or person dealing with Baltimore or Maryland. One of the favorite subjects suggested by readers has been a reminiscence of the fire. Probably nearly twenty have been published since the Magazine started that feature in 1949. Two are reproduced.

Even in the 1970's — years after the fire — as the February anniversary approached, readers would bring in or send to the Magazine mementoes of the fire. The most popular were age-stained and brittle pages of newspapers of that time, copies of the souvenir books published after the fire, and old photographs. Most of the pictures were taken after the fire, and with few exceptions were duplicates of ones that have been reproduced many times. Of the hundreds of pictures that I have examined in the past twenty-five years, not one turned out to be a good picture taken during the fire or a different view of the aftermath. The few excellent pictures that were made during the fire are reproduced in "Baltimore Afire."

In looking back with the perspective of 75 years to the catastrophe of 1904, the recovery that Baltimore made is not only an astonishing but an almost unbelievable achievement. The five skyscrapers that were gutted were rebuilt within a year. Bigger and grander buildings replaced those that were destroyed. All this was accomplished by a city relying not on massive Federal assistance, but just its own resources.

But over the years most of those new office buildings and warehouses rushed to completion in 1904 and 1905 became outmoded if not dilapidated. There were increasing vacancies, falling rents, eroding values. The wooden structures that had served as passenger and freight terminals and warehouses along the waterfront on Pratt and Light Streets had outlived their times as busses and trucks replaced the bay steamers that had once crowded the inner harbor. Since most of these buildings looked like they were about to tumble down, the city had them demolished and the northwest corner of the waterfront made into a park honoring Sam Smith, a hero of the War of 1812 and a former mayor of Baltimore.

The Associated Press reported, "The 1950's found downtown Baltimore, like the center of many other American cities, a very sick patient. Buildings were decaying. Property taxes were down. Retail sales were down. There hadn't been a new hotel in thirty years or a new theater in forty years. Major building activity was almost nonexistent in the heart of the city."

In 1954 the Committee for Downtown, composed of business leaders, and the Greater Baltimore Committee financed a $225,000 plan for the renewal of the business district bounded by Centre Street, the harbor, the Fallsway and Greene Street. But it soon became obvious that by the time such an ambitious plan could be implemented much of the downtown area would be beyond help. A new plan was drawn up for the redevelopment of the downtown core, between the retail and financial districts. The area, bounded by Saratoga, Charles, Lombard and Liberty Streets and Hopkins Place, covered much of the area devastated by the fire on Sunday afternoon, February 7. J. Jefferson Miller, a retired department store executive who had been instrumental in raising money for the 1954 survey, became the $1 a year man in charge of Charles Center, the name given to the project.

It covered 33 acres and was estimated to cost $130,000,000. The city agreed to undertake the project as part of its urban renewal program.

A special session of the Maryland legislature voted to put the question of a $35,000,000 urban renewal loan on the ballot in November, 1958. It was approved and by the following year acquisition of the 350 properties in the area began. Five of the original buildings were kept, but many landmarks disappeared: O'Neill's Department Store, the Century and Valencia movie theaters on Lexington Street, Miller Brothers Restaurant on Fayette Street and the Sun Building at Charles and Baltimore Streets.

Ground for the first building, One Charles Center, was broken in August, 1961. The 24-story dark glass and smoky aluminum office tower was designed by the noted German-born architect, Mies van der Rohe. When it was completed in October, 1962 it was hailed as a masterpiece of design. The three-story buff-colored brick and glass building of Hamburger's apparel store was completed the next year, spanning Fayette Street and joining the plaza of One Charles Center. In September, 1964 the seven-story glass and stainless steel Vermont Federal Building on Fayette Street was opened.

In 1966 the Gas and Electric Company wrapped an annex around two sides of its headquarters building at Lexington and Liberty Streets. The same year the Sun Life Insurance Company of America finished a new home office, a 12-story black granite and glass tower on Charles Street south of Redwood Street.

Three major buildings were finished in 1967:

The $18,700,000 Federal Office Building is a 17-story granite and aluminum building which at night, with some of its windows illuminated, strikes many observers as "an IBM card with some of its holes punched." The Hilton Hotel is a 23-story tower with 350 rooms. The Morris A. Mechanic Theatre claims to be the first private theater built since World War I. It seats 1,800 and was constructed of board-marked concrete. The low structure, in sharp contrast to the tall buildings around it, was designed by John M. Johansen in the style of "functional expressionism" — without the usual geometrical exterior covering interior shapes. At first the building was widely criticized, but it is now regarded as one of the Center's architectural gems.

Then came Two Charles Center, a shopping and residential complex of two towers, the Fidelity Building annex, the 24-story Mercantile Safe

Deposit and Trust Building, a second tower for the Hilton Hotel with 250 guest rooms and a ballroom, and, in 1975, Charles Center South, a major office building just south of the Sun Life Building.

Charles Center, which has given Baltimore a new skyline, has above-street walkways that connect buildings at varying levels, and three landscaped plazas. The one in front of the Federal Building is called Hopkins Plaza. It is dominated by a spraying fountain given in memory of Jacob France. On pleasant days the plaza is filled with strollers and office workers eating lunch at cafes along one side of the Mechanic Theatre building. The plaza also becomes an open air stage for a variety of special events held during the day and evening. The oval-shaped Center Plaza, with many benches and an expanse of lawn, lies between One Charles Center and the Gas and Electric Company buildings. Beneath these plazas, and the one of Two Charles Center, are underground garages for nearly 2,000 vehicles.

Charles Center cost about $180,000,000, most of which came from the private economy. Public expenditures of about $39,000,000 were used to buy and clear the land and create settings that would attract private capital. The fifteen major buildings contribute about $3,000,000 annually in real estate taxes, some six times what was collected from that area in 1958. And, perhaps even more significantly, the number of people in Charles Center — those working, living and visiting — has tripled in the last nine years.

The Center has won a number of national awards, both for the project itself and for the architectural excellence of some of its buildings. The *New York Times* in a comprehensive article on Baltimore in 1967 said, "This is a city that is lifting itself by the seat of its pants. A 33-acre section of rundown buildings, the threadbare fabric between its two major pockets of commerce, has been replaced by one of the nation's most successful downtown projects."

Now Charles Center is the hub of a network of several projects. Along its edges are other buildings that have added to the new look of downtown Baltimore. Facing the southern side — close to where the Great Fire began — is the Civic Center. The $14,000,000 structure, opened in 1962, has a 10,000-seat sports arena and coliseum, plus exhibi-

Aerial view looking across the Inner Harbor to the Baltimore skyline. The old cluttered harbor basin has been redeveloped as a dramatic gateway to the city. Contrast this vista with the photographs on Pages 52-53.

tion space. Facing the eastern side on Charles Street are the Blaustein Building and the Arlington Federal Building.

With Charles Center almost complete, attention turned to the Inner Harbor area, some of which was part of the Burnt District of 1904.

The city government asked Mr. Miller and Martin Millspaugh to undertake the planning and implementation. Mr. Millspaugh, a Baltimore newspaperman who had served as assistant commissioner of the U.S. Urban Renewal Administration, had been deputy manager of Charles Center since 1960. They agreed and formed the non-profit corporation known as Charles Center-Inner Harbor Management, Inc. Mr. Miller died in 1972 and Mr. Millspaugh subsequently became president and chief executive officer.

The plan is to make the Inner Harbor a dramatic gateway to the central business district and to return the shoreline, for years obscured by waterfront structures, to public use.

A promenade, paved with brick to reflect Baltimore's traditional use of brick, follows the northern and western edges of the harbor. Fairs, festivals, concerts and celebrations are held along its reaches. During the day and early evening strollers and sightseers enjoy its vistas. A focal point on the northern side of the harbor is Constellation Dock where the U.S.F. *Constellation*, the oldest fighting ship in the Navy, is moored. It is a sightseeing attraction and a historic and romantic reminder of Baltimore's part in American maritime life.

To the east is the World Trade Center. Designed by the noted architectural firm, I.M. Pei and Associates, the 32-story office tower rises 430 feet above the water. The top floor was planned as a roof-top restaurant and enclosed observation tower which offers a marvelous view of the harbor and, on a clear day, a vista of the Chesapeake Bay. From the water the pentagon-shape of the building looks like a huge prow looming above the harbor.

At the northwest corner of Pratt and Light Streets the United States Fidelity and Guaranty Company built a 40-story home office building. Just east of it is an office building for the International Business Machines Corporation. South of the United States Fidelity & Guaranty Building is a headquarters office building for the Chesapeake and Potomac Tele-

90

phone Company. On the southwest corner of the Inner Harbor is the Maryland Science Center which includes a science museum, planetarium and exhibition space of the Maryland Academy of Sciences. To the west is the complex of Christ Lutheran Church which contains a 220-bed nursing home, 288 apartments for the elderly and a public plaza with underground parking.

Scheduled for completion in late 1979 or early 1980 is the Aquarium on Pier 3 Pratt Street which will display marine life in a natural habitat.

In the November, 1978 elections Baltimore voters approved the Harborplace project, two steel and glass pavilions to house 140 businesses, mostly eating places. The pavilions will be built at the northwest corner of the Inner Harbor by the Rouse Company at a cost of $15,000,000.

That same month plans were discussed for a hotel to be built by the Hyatt Hotel Corporation. The site would be on Light Street between the C. & P. Telephone Company and the McCormick and Company Building, one of three buildings that remained in the area. The hotel would have a 5-story atrium with a plant and tree-filled lobby. Four capsule-shaped glass elevators, with views of the harbor, would serve the 13-story hotel. Most of the 500 rooms would have a view of the inner harbor area.

The second stage of development of the area is called Inner Harbor West. It includes the new Federal Courthouse and office building in the block at the northwest corner of Pratt and Hanover Streets, the Convention Center, bounded by Pratt, Charles, Camden and Sharp Streets, the Equitable Bank Center at the Southwest corner of Charles and Lombard Streets, and a high rise structure for the elderly.

This is the *new* Baltimore that gives the city a new look and a bright future — a new downtown and Inner Harbor complex that, for the most part, has been built where downtown Baltimore lay in smoldering ruins just 75 years ago.

I Remember When . . .

At 12 I Covered the Great Baltimore Fire of 1904

Mr. Simpson

By E. Ridgely Simpson

ABOUT this time 55 years ago I was taking up a cash collection to send to the mother of one of the two firemen who lost their lives as a result of the Baltimore fire in 1904.

The fire, you may recall, was discovered shortly before noon on Sunday, February 7, in the basement of the John E. Hurst & Co. building on what is now Redwood street, between Hopkins place and Liberty street. An explosion there spread the fire, which raged for 30 hours and destroyed more than 1,500 buildings over some 140 acres of downtown and waterfront areas. The loss was estimated around $100,000,000.

. More than 1,500 firefighters—members of the Baltimore department, some 400 unattached volunteers and units which sped from Philadelphia, New York, Washington and other surrounding towns and cities, probably a dozen in all—finally brought the fire under control.

Having seen the fire, I still think it is a great miracle that nobody was killed in it. There were two firemen, however, who died later because of it.

Engineer Mark Kelly, of New York's Engine Company No. 16, returned to New York on February 9 with a bad cold contracted during 22 hours of duty in Baltimore. Pneumonia developed and he died on February 26.

Pipeman James Montgomery McGlennen, of Baltimore Engine Company No. 7, Eutaw street and Druid Hill avenue, also contracted pneumonia from exposure during the fire and died. His funeral was held on March 10.

I WAS 22 in 1904 and, as far as I know, the youngest newspaper reporter to cover the big fire. Shortly after Christmas that year, I might explain, I had launched a little hectographed newspaper called the Boy's Home Journal, which several chums and I turned out weekly at my home, a four-story brick building at 6 East Read street that has since been torn down and replaced by an apartment building.

I was reporter, advertising salesman, delivery boy, editor and publisher. Other staff members were kids who lived right around the neighborhood and friends from the schools we attended.

Jerome Vogler was our cartoonist. The late William T. Dixon, who was to become my brother-in-law, Donald Price and D'Arcy Didier were reporters. Mary Camilla McKim (now Mrs. Huntington Williams) contributed children's stories, mostly about her pet white rabbit, which she often took walking on a leash.

We charged 5 cents a copy, which was five times what The Sun got for its paper. We sold our crudely drawn ads throughout the neighborhood—to Dunlop's Oyster House, Corcoran's Livery Stable and Mr. Jacobs, the tailor, on Richmond street; to Mr. Cook, the florist, and to Thomas M. Reese, the grocer, on Charles street.

We covered the usual neighborhood news—lost dogs, found dogs, school items. Once I published an epic poem I had written about a scrap out at Country School, a scrap in which Louis Merryman and Pard Vogler stood off a whole pack of other kids.

We were an established newspaper

with four or five weeks of experience when the big fire of 1904 came along. At first, on Sunday night, I was too busy being a fireman to bother with gathering the news. My father and I spent most of the night up on our roof throwing water on the big firebrands that fell there.

I spent the next day skirting the fringes of the still raging fire, "covering" it for our newspaper. On Calvert street, down around Mercy Hospital, I remember, I rushed up to a woman and began brushing vigorously at her hat when I saw a firebrand land on her. The poor woman must have thought I was a purse snatcher, for she whirled around and gave me a stinging backhand slap.

Our little paper came out in due time with my story of the fire. Later, when we heard that Fireman McGlennen had died, we began taking up our collection.

HERE are the contributors on my list:

Morris Hall, 50 cents; D'Arcy Didier, 30 cents; Donald Pierce, $1.50; John Stewart, 25 cents; Edward S. Clark, 20 cents; Lee Packard, 4 cents; Frank Carey, 30 cents; James Manning, 5 cents; Allan Smith, $2; George Williams, 25 cents; J. Marshall Thomas, Jr., 10 cents; Allan McLane, 25 cents; James Bruce, 25 cents; William Dixon, 25 cents; Jack Archer, 10 cents; Philip Archer, 10 cents; Roswell Josephs, 25 cents; L. H. Buckler, 25 cents.

F. F. Reid, 25 cents; Charles D. F. Brune, 25 cents; Dr. Mackenzie, 25 cents; Este Fisher, 25 cents; Louis M. L. Fisher, 25 cents; Edward Martin, $1; Frederic X. Williams, 10 cents; John Winslow Williams, 10 cents; Juliana Keyser, 25 cents; McHenry Kerper, 25 cents; Ross Whistler, 50 cents; William Keyser Manly, 50 cents; David K. E. Bruce, 25 cents; William Cabell Bruce, Jr., 25 cents; Reginald and Preston Petre, 20 cents; Washington Platt, 25 cents; the Misses Trimble, 50 cents; O'Donovan, 30 cents; Bonsal, 75 cents; Petri, 20 cents.

Mary Camilla McKim, $2.75; Margaret Carey, 50 cents; Elizabeth Jencks, 25 cents; Eleanor Jencks, 25 cents; Lydia H. Deford, 25 cents; Nancy M. Deford, 25 cents; Mary Ridgely Preston, 10 cents; Emily S. Riggs, $1; Ethel McLane Lee, 25 cents; Katharine S. Lee, 25 cents; Elinor McLane, 25 cents; Leslie Buckler, 10 cents; Marian Bond, 25 cents; Mary Josephs, 25 cents; Louise Murdoch, 25 cents; Gretchen Williams, 10 cents; Mary Cushing Williams, 10 cents; Doris Reid, 25 cents.

Nancy Fisher Brune, $1; Louise E. Fisher, 25 cents; Sophia M. L. Fisher, 25 cents; Katy, 25 cents; Anne Winslow Williams, 10 cents; Ellen Keyser, 25 cents; Misses Tunstall Smith, 20 cents; Strother, 30 cents; Mrs. Frank Turner, $1; Mrs. Thomas Morris, $1; J. Swan Frick, 50 cents; Charles Field, 50 cents; Lt. Cmdr. Simpson (my father), $1; collected in banks around town, 57 cents; myself, $3; anonymous, 50 cents. The grand total was $31.66.

James McGlennen, above, who developed pneumonia, was the only Baltimorean to lose his life as a result of the great 1904 fire, a scene from which is shown at left.

E. Ridgely Simpson wrote a report of the fire for a paper he edited and published when he was 12. Many Baltimoreans have written first person accounts of the fire for the "I Remember" feature of the Baltimore Sun Magazine.

I Remember . . .
. . . Baltimore's Thank-You Parade

By Benjamin W. Weaver

Deputy Chief, Washington Fire Department (Ret.)

IN the late summer of 1906, two years after the great fire, all of the out-of-town companies that had helped fight it were invited by Baltimore city to come back for a huge parade during the Baltimore Jubilee.

We had to get up at dawn that morning of September 13 in order to load our five engines and fifteen horses on a train in Union Station by 9 o'clock. In Baltimore we joined nearly 1,400 other firemen in the parade that lasted over two hours. We didn't get back to Washington until nearly midnight; then we paraded from the Peace Monument down to Fifteenth street before bedding our horses and ourselves down for the night. We did all this on what must have been the hottest day of 1906.

I was a sergeant in No. 2 Engine at the time. The other companies that had gone over in 1904 were Numbers 3, 6, 7 and 8, of ten men each. In charge was Chief Engineer William T. Belt.

For the 1906 trip to Baltimore we loaded our spic-and-span engines on flat cars and put the horses in a boxcar. We rode in a coach. We arrived about 10 o'clock at Camden Station, unloaded and moved to the assembly area on South Broadway. There was hardly room to turn around there. Men, women and children were pushing and crowding around us, looking at the apparatus and admiring our horses.

By noon we were beginning to feel the heat. We were wearing our dress uniforms, which consisted of heavy trousers and a heavy, lined coat almost like an overcoat. Yet we were more fortunate than some, in that we were wearing our caps while they had on heavy fire helmets. The fire commissioners didn't look too comfortable, either, in their frock-coats, striped pants and tall silk hats.

We were supposed to step off at 2 o'clock, but one of the out-of-town units had some trouble getting its equipment off the train and we had to stand around and wait. There were firemen all over South Broadway as we formed up. There were three companies from Annapolis, 75 men from Philadelphia, nearly 60 from Atlantic City, 60 from Wilmington and some from Harrisburg, York, Chester, Westminster and other Maryland towns, along with practically the entire Baltimore force.

The crowds grew bigger, and just before the start somebody threw a big bunch of carnations on the chief's wagon. We stepped out, and in spite of the heat, everybody looked well. The uniforms of firemen and bandsmen from nearly twenty bands were smart and colorful, axes and brass on the apparatus gleamed, horses pranced smartly along—many of them with tails and manes plaited for the occasion.

Each piece of apparatus had a silk guidon, and on the houses and buildings there were streamers and flags flying. People were cheering all along the way, waving handkerchiefs and throwing cigarettes, cigars and peanuts at us as we rolled along.

WE moved west on Baltimore street, where the picture on this page was taken. Then we went by City Hall, where a reviewing stand was set up. Most of the out-of-towners didn't recognize Gov. Edwin Warfield and Mayor E. Clay Timanus on the stand, and those who did not tip their hats as they passed the stand were hooted by a group of about 100 small boys who were having a lot of fun.

From City Hall we paraded through what was called the Burnt District up to Howard street, then up to Monument street and across to Mount Vernon place, where we broke up.

The heat of the day had reached most of us before we even got to City Hall. All along the line of march you could see men lifting off their caps and helmets and mopping their brows.

When the horses began to look droopy around the ears, about halfway through the parade, we had to stop and let them drink. Then several times we'd have to refresh them by dousing their heads with buckets of water. One of our men, Frank Clements, was overcome by the heat while we were forming up, and Capt. John Carrington jumped into the Baltimore chief's wagon and rushed off for a doctor.

WHEN it was over, some of the companies attended a big celebration for them at Electric Park that evening and stayed overnight. We in the Washington group were scheduled to get home by 6 in the evening, however. As it happened, there was a delay in loading our equipment on the train and we all had to go to a restaurant near the station for dinner. We didn't get back to Union Station until 11 o'clock.

We had been scheduled to parade again, but because of the late hour and the tiredness of horses and men, it wasn't much of a parade. We were in a hurry to get back to our firehouses. There was only a handful of people on the street to see us, anyway.

During the 33 hours we were in Baltimore in 1904 fighting the great fire, we didn't suffer a single casualty. But as a result of the Jubilee heat and excitement, we had one man overcome and lost two horses. Engine 6 and Engine 8 each lost one. They died shortly after we got back.

Washington fire companies that helped to fight the great 1904 fire parading on Baltimore street during the Baltimore Jubilee held in 1906.

2

Our Readers Write

Horse Gets A Ride

TO THE EDITOR OF THE MAGA-ZINE—*Sir:* Inclosed is a snapshot picture of a horse-drawn streetcar which was taken in 1895.

Mr. Martin J. Mack, 1735 Montpelier street, Baltimore, gave me the picture. Mr. Mack said an old man—whose name he has forgotten—gave him the picture many years ago.

The streetcar was horsedrawn, but after reaching the end of his trudge upward the horse proceeded to board the trolley and then, presumably, keenly enjoyed his ride back down the hill. In the picture

the horse appears to be about to alight—or dismount—or disembark — whichever term is most correct in describing a horse getting off a streetcar.

Mr. Mack told me that he was told the location of the picture was "Cherrieville," in the Brooklyn region of South Baltimore suburbs.

LOUIS P. TRUE.
Glen Burnie, Md.

[EDITOR'S NOTE — The only Cherrieville we can discover is a suburb of Denver, Col.]

The Old Tobaccos

TO THE EDITOR OF THE MAGA-ZINE—*Sir:* As proprietor of a tobacco shop in Baltimore, I still sell many of the early brands of tobacco that were mentioned in Raymond Kamzler's article "When Cigarettes Were Young." For instance, Piedmont and Sweet Caporal cigarettes, Schnapps and Brown's Mule chewing tobaccos, Five Brothers, Picnic Twist, Mail Pouch, Bull Durham, Duke's Mixture. Also clay pipes and corncobs, and the cigarette-making machines.

Until a few years ago. Recruits were still available, and likewise the Golden Crown cigars advertised on the base of the wooden Indian in the picture that accompanied the article. I believe that the Pittsburg stogie can still be bought. I stock the Marsh Wheeling stogie, a brand that is probably older than I am.

As for snuff, it is still widely used by young and old, by males and females.

HERMAN ROSKES.
4114 Fernhill avenue.

OUR PICTURES

Cover—Sunpaper photo, A. Aubrey Bodine.
Pages 6, 7—Fairchild Aerial Surveys, Inc.
Page 8—Sunpaper photo, Bodine.
Pages 11 to 13 — Sunpaper photos, Bodine.
Page 15—Sunpaper photo, Bodine.
Page 18—Baltimore Museum of Art; Sunpaper photos, Charles Purcell, Junior.
Page 21 — Sunpaper artist, John Stees.

Benjamin W. Weaver, retired deputy chief of the Washington Fire Department, recalls the "thank you parade" when out-of-town fire companies which fought the 1904 fire were invited back for a parade and celebration.

ACKNOWLEDGMENTS

"Once I had caught up on lost sleep I prepared to do a narrative on the fire as I had seen it, with whatever help I could get from the other *Herald* men, but the project got itself postponed so often that I finally abandoned it, and to this day no connected story has ever been printed."

Henry L. Mencken wrote that sentence in 1941 for his book, "Newspaper Days."

This account, written thirteen years after the Mencken statement and fifty years after the fire, is, if nothing else, the first connected story of the fire and its aftermath ever printed in book form.

A great many people — including Mencken — had a hand in making it possible.

The author is particularly indebted to:

Frank F. Dorsey, vice president and director of the Fire-Marine Department of the United States Fidelity & Guaranty Company, who first suggested a fiftieth anniversary book about the fire.

C. William Schneidereith, Sr. who edited the book and whose talent, experience and enthusiasm have been of great help on every page.

Richard C. Sheridan who, with patience and unfailing good humor, worked hard and well, seven days a week, on everything from the title to the acknowledgment page.

Hervey Brackbill, once again, for his kindness in reading the manuscript and for making many valuable suggestions.

Pinkney W. Wilkinson, secretary of the Fire Board and a participant in the Great Fire, for answering question after question over a period of many months; John Kahl, a retired deputy fire chief and the first fireman to enter the burning Hurst Building, for his vivid recollections of that Sunday morning; F. Albert Roloson and his brother, Charles H. Roloson, Jr., for their detailed and colorful descriptions and wonderful anecdotes;

Harry A. Donahoo, a retired fire lieutenant, for his account of a fireman's view of the two-day conflagration; George B. C. Miller, superintendent of the City's Property Location Division, for searching through forgotten records and maps; John H. Mintiens, a retired police inspector, for his description of police activities in 1904; Arthur L. Keigler, treasurer of the Baltimore Equitable Society, for his help; Frank R. Kent, Abraham Cole, John N. Richardson, John Rohm, and many, many others whose reminiscences found a place in this book.

The girls of the Maryland Room of the Enoch Pratt Library — especially Miss Howard Hubbard — for their amazing ability to locate anything and everything.

Employees of the Fire Department, the Police Department, the Department of Legislative Reference, the office of the State Insurance Commissioner, the Washington Fire Department, the *Sunpapers'* Library, and the office of Municipal Archives, for making available records, books and files.

Mr. Dorsey, who is also president of the Insurance Historical Society of Baltimore, for the use of the society's records and the pictures from the Jacob Gross Collection; the Pratt Library for permission to use many of its pictures; J. H. Schaefer & Son for the remarkable pictures from the J. William Schaefer Collection; and Wilbur Hunter, director of the Peale Museum, for his work in locating many fine old pictures and his permission to use them.

Alfred A. Knopf, Inc., New York, for permission to reproduce excerpts from "Newspaper Days" by H. L. Mencken.

And, twenty-five years later . . .
Once again, Clement G. Vitek, chief librarian of the *Sunpapers'* Library and his assistants for their help.

Charles Center–Inner Harbor Management, Inc., for providing illustrations used in the Epilogue.

C. William Schneidereith, Jr., for republishing "Baltimore Afire" twenty-five years after his father published the first edition, and for his help and suggestions in all aspects of this new edition.